Lynn Wilkinson resides in Sherwood Park, Alberta where she has been a Realtor for 25 years. Lynn has a son and a daughter and 5 grandchildren. This is the first book for her but her poetry has been published previously

Cover Photo: North Vancouver, 2012.

Lynn Wilkinson

Mystic Lights Publishing
West 4th Avenue RPO
PO Box 19173
Vancouver, B.C. Canada
www.mysticlightspublishing.com

ISBN: 978-0-9784986-6-5

24 23 22 21 20 19 18 17 16   1 2 3 4 5

DEDICATION

This book is for my Mom and Dad.

LIST OF POEMS

PREFACE

For several years now, I have had a feeling within that I needed to write a book containing all the poetry I have channeled and the stories behind them. It has taken me quite some time to get this undertaking started mainly because I have a Master's Degree in Procrastination. I am discipline challenged plus I am a Pisces. While one fish is focused and motivated to do what it takes to move forward, the other fish wants to perfect the art of doing nothing bringing stillness to my mind. It has been an interesting journey to close the door on the past thirteen year cycle and to bring this book to LIGHT.

ACKNOWLEDGMENTS

Thank you to friends and family who have chosen to love and support me just as I am

I was born on February 24, 1950 in the Wainwright Hospital in central Alberta and was raised on a farm southeast of Wainwright, close to a small town named Edgerton. I don't have a lot of memories from my childhood but do have one very old memory that has never left me. It is of being very scared, not knowing where I was, and not knowing why everything was different. I remember a feeling of being very alone. I used to think when I woke up in the morning that I would be back where I felt safe but it never happened. I have a very vague memory of standing by the washing machine while mom was washing clothes. I was feeling comforted by the sound and vibration of the motor and asked my mom if I could go back. She didn't understand what I was talking about and told me not to be silly and to keep my fingers away from the wringer.

These early thoughts and experiences were brought to light for me in 1992 when I went to see a chiropractor that Treva, one of my oldest and closest friends, told me about. This practitioner also saw and read body auras. She was very excited about this doctor and thought I would be interested in meeting with him. So I made an appointment.

He asked me to sit in a chair then he turned the lights out. A minute later he turned them back on and said he needed to change his schedule since I would take more than an hour's time. He left the room and returned a few minutes later and explained that he wanted me to lay on his table and be still. He said that he could see auras and my life as it had unfolded.

He started by saying that I was one of the few people he had ever seen with no breaks in their aura which meant no baggage. He then told me that I was separated from my parents at a very young age and it was a spiritual separation. As soon as he said that, I remembered my feelings as a child, of being lost and wanting to go back. I remembered feeling myself being pulled away from my mother, knowing that my parents would love me but never know me. When the session was over I felt much lighter as if a weight was lifted from me. These same old memories were brought to the light once again in 2013. The second of my oldest, closest friends is Shari. Shari, Treva, and I grew up together, so we have been best friends for over fifty-five years. We have laughed, cried and weathered many storms together. I count on these two strong and funny women when I need to unload. They have always been there for me and I will be eternally grateful for their friendship and wisdom, along with their humour which has never let me down. There's nothing that a glass of wine, a good friend, and a good laugh won't ease.

In May of 2013 Shari was in Edmonton from Victoria to visit her sister, Caroline. We were sitting in the kitchen reminiscing about our years growing up in Edgerton and I suddenly found myself telling her about this old memory of being very scared, not knowing where I was, and wanting to go back. Shari then told me a story her mom told her when she was in the Palliative Care Unit in the Wainwright Hospital. Shari's mom was a teacher in Edgerton School for many years. Her mom said that I would find her at recess and holding her hand would walk around the grounds. During one of those walks, I told her that I really didn't belong here. I was really an Indian and was waiting for someone to come and take me back. I have no memories of this but as Shari was telling the story, I could feel the fear and confusion I had in those years. As I got older these feelings diminished but they have never totally gone away. I have always had a sense of "knowing" things and have always felt the light that was within me. Even as a young child there was an awareness of another "me" and I knew that this "me" was my protection and guide. It would be another three decades before I started learning about the "higher self." Like most of the farmers in the area, my parents worked very hard to make a living and money was always in short supply. We had no electricity or running water but did have a big lake behind our house that provided much fun in winter and summer.

My father raised cattle, horses, pigs, chickens, and turkeys. Mom had a huge garden and there were many fruit trees, so we always had good healthy food. It was a time of hard work morning to night and the comforts we take for granted today didn't exist. My mom cooked on a wood and coal stove which along with an oil stove provided heat in the winter. In the summer, mom cooked in a shed so the house wouldn't get so hot. Life then was hard but simple.

I had two older brothers and two younger. My oldest brother lived in Edmonton so I only saw him when he visited. My second oldest was seven years older than me and the two younger were very close in age to me so my mom had her hands full. My dad was a very quiet man and I don't remember his ever swearing. I only saw him angry a couple of times and that was during cattle round up and branding season which was always stressful. Dad seemed to always have a smile and had the most beautiful blue eyes that seemed to smile too. He seemed to know something the rest of us didn't and he was the most grounded, non-judgmental person I have ever known.

Although dad was not educated beyond grade eight and he had never experienced anything but the farm he possessed a wisdom that school could not teach. I got my love of animals and nature from him.

Mom was the one who disciplined and she did swear but it was in Gaelic so we never knew what she was saying. She was a very strong woman and tended to be a bit of a loner. She enjoyed people when they were around but was just fine on her own. In later years it was only mom and dad on the farm and she suffered from depression although no one knew it. If my father was the grounding force for me, my mother was the strength and wisdom. Neither my mom nor my dad complained . . . just did what needed to be done. My mom always had the radio on so we grew up with music as a big part of our lives.

Entertainment for my parents and the other farmers was at the community hall dances. There was no such thing as baby sitters so the kids were taken and when they got tired they slept under the pile of coats that were piled on the stage not far from the musicians. My brother, Bill, became an accomplished musician and singer. I attempted to learn the guitar but didn't and still don't have my brother's discipline. I can, however, whistle and, quite well if I do say so.

To this day I have a CD playing when I go to bed and find the music very comforting. As a little girl I was afraid of everything and everyone. I loved being outside and spent hours with my dad since mom had her hands full with two little boys. When my older brother got home from school, I would be with him.

If you were to ask my brothers if I was spoiled or the

favorite, they would all say "yes." I was the only girl, so in their eyes I was spoiled and I was. But I think it was because both mom and dad thought there was something wrong with me. The only thing mom ever told me about myself as a child was that Bill rocked me for hours when I was sick with scarlet fever and that I was always with him when he was home from school. She said that I was happiest when outside and also told me that when Bill graduated and left for Edmonton, I was lost and didn't talk for a long time. My friends and family will find that hard to believe as would any of the older generation in Edgerton. I loved talking to older people and my school bus driver called me Windy not Lyndy which explains a lot. I would have been eleven at the time and still remember feeling lost without Bill. I was the happiest riding my horse, especially if I was out in the hills where I felt most at home. The hills was a huge tract of land with trees, sand hills, small lakes, and places were water just bubbled out of the ground to form springs. At one time thousands of buffalo roamed the area but the last of them were rounded up and shipped to Elk Island Park in the 1930's. This land belonged to the federal government and was used as a training ground for the military stationed at Wainwright Army Base. Our farm backed onto this land and in the spring and summer cattle were allowed onto these lands as long as the cattle owners belonged to the Wainwright Grazing Association.

As I got older my cousin, who lived a few miles away; my brother, Bill; and myself would be hired to move cattle from farms to the grazing pastures. These are wonderful memories . . . long days in the saddle with very sore butts but such an incredible feeling of freedom. This is where I felt most at home and the least lost.

I didn't particularly enjoy school although I do have some great memories such as M.B. sticking my long braids in his ink bottle and then laughing. It was my turn to laugh when the teacher got hold of him. One thing I did know once I started school was that the other "me" was not something I could share with anyone so I never did. Even as a child I knew that this other "me" was there to protect and guide me. I came to understand that this "me" was the one who "knew" stuff and "felt" things. I have always known that my thoughts, feelings, words, and actions would register on a "light bar" within me and this was, in a way, an inner guidance system that has directed my whole life.

My mom and dad were not religious, so we never went to church. My first experience with church was one Sunday when I had stayed with a friend named Lynne, who lived in town. As soon as I walked into the church I felt different. Today I would say that I felt a change in the energy and vibration around me. At that time I just felt different. I always felt a light or glow in my tummy and when I sat down in that church it seemed that my "light" got brighter. It was an amazing feeling and I was wondering what was going to happen in this church.

As it turned out, this was my introduction to "God" and "Jesus." I didn't know who they were but the words were so powerful for me. This began my love of words and the awareness of their power. "God" and "Jesus" opened a world of questions.

I had another friend, who lived north of town and I spent weekends with her once in awhile. Her family went to church, although it was different than the one I went to in town. Once again I felt different and the words resonated with me, I loved these stories and wanted to know more about this book called a Bible. I found that the questions I asked in my mind were soon answered. Although I had no idea of the source, I knew that they were the truth and came through the other "me."This brought a huge amount of comfort and I began to feel less alone.

One of my earliest visions was of a huge oval table and an energy at opposite ends. . One was a white glow and the other was black. The white glow gave me a good feeling but the black scared me. I didn't understand what this meant, but I did know it was important. As I got older and became more aware, I came to think of this table as having God at one end and Satan at the other. This image has come back to me many times over the years and at these times I would question the relationship between God and Satan. Answers were slow to come but they did come. I came to understand that the relationship was far more complex than what the Church taught.

These question and answer periods have continued throughout my life and in August 2013 I was guided to a book called, Outwitting the Devil. It was written by Napoleon Hill who is best known for his book, Think and Grow Rich which he wrote in 1937. Outwitting the Devil was written in 1938 but his wife didn't want it published because of the devil's role in it. It wasn't until the Napoleon Hill Foundation asked Sharon Lechter to edit the manuscript that the book came to light. It was finally released in June 2011. The book was a huge gift because in it I saw myself . . .all the questions I had asked over the years were here. I connected with the author in a huge way because here was a person who thought like me.

The summer that I was fourteen I went to Edmonton to work for my dad's sister who owned a restaurant on

124th Street. I got to experience a life that was far different from the one on the farm or in my little home town of Edgerton. I enjoyed working and felt really good knowing that I would be going home with money in the bank. I worked the following two summers in the city as well and explored the areas around 124th Street. I was drawn to the river valley and the Glenora area spending hours walking in the trees along the river and along sidewalks in front of the beautiful homes. I felt very at home and that feeling has never left me. Today when I'm stressed I head for the trails along the river and still find peace and comfort there. There is powerful energy in this area and it is here that I received some of my most powerful messages.

I finished school in 1968 and went to work in the Wainwright Bank of Montreal. On August 2, 1968 I got married to my best friend and someone I loved since I was fifteen when he "bought" me in my grade nine initiation. I had to dress as a slave that day and then had to work for him all day Saturday before the Initiation Dance. I weeded his mom's garden, helped her do some things in the house, and listened to his youngest brother, Martin, tell me jokes from his new 1001 Elephant Jokes.

Our son, Shannon, was born in 1970 and our daughter, Tara, in 1975. We spent every weekend going home to Edgerton and split our time between my parent's place and his parent,s place. This was something all the kids we grew up with did. By the time Tara was born we had moved to Sherwood Park. My brother Bill, his wife, Darlene, and their two boys followed us to the Park as did my oldest brother, Terry and his wife, Leona.

We all continued to go home to the farm for Christmas, Easter, and Thanksgiving and it was wonderful chaos. My four brothers and myself bought mom and dad a mobile home in 1972 and they had water and sewer put in. This was luxury compared to the old farm house. Although it was crowded and noisy, some of my best memories are of the times we were all together. My youngest brother, Wayne, got married in 1979 and took over the farm. Mom and dad moved to Wainwright where they spent their remaining years. The family gatherings for Christmas, Easter, and Thanksgiving continued and the numbers grew as more grand-children came along.

During these years I was a busy mom and also worked full time at the Royal Bank. God was still on my mind a lot and I was fascinated with the human mind. I knew how mine worked but often wondered if everyone else's worked in the same way. My brother, Bill, was who I turned to for answers and advise.

With all the ugly details of the Viet Nam War making headlines I had become very angry and often questioned the existence of a God. What we were told about the war was far removed from the truth of it. Thousands upon thousands of soldiers and innocent people on both sides paid with their lives but there were some men who made millions of dollars from this war. The rest of their lives were spent walking on the bones of the dead with $$$$ in their pockets but few ever were brought to justice. It was a hard time for me and I frustrated Bill with my blocked mind and angry judgment of God and mankind, especially governments.

The birth of my daughter was a catalyst for renewing my belief although that came along with unending questions for which I struggled to find answers. Because I questioned constantly I blocked my own spiritual development. I knew there was another "me" and never questioned the existence of this. However I wanted concrete answers to many, many questions that had none. It took decades for me to evolve beyond acceptance and belief to a place of Faith. Faith is believing when it is beyond reason to believe. I had made progress (and I had helped in the distinguished graying of my brother's hair . . . at least he didn't lose his hair!).

I have always had people ask if they could talk to me and have always been able to tell them what they needed to hear at that time. I never doubted where this information came from nor did I doubt its validity; however, I was cautious and made sure they understood what the message was. I have always been willing to help others as long as they were willing to help themselves. There is no free ride and no quick fix, we all have to do our own work. No angel or guide is going to do it for us . . .they can show the way if we are open and listening but we must do the hard work it takes in order to evolve and awaken.

We often stand in our own way but we can't overcome the obstacle if we don't take responsibility for it's creation. Easy to say but harder to do. One of my favorite quotes is from Victor Hugo, "A man is not idle because he is absorbed in thought. There is visible labor and there is invisible labor." Awakening is invisible labor done within and showing the visible results in our actions, our thoughts, and our words.

The 1980's found me reading whatever books I was guided to read. The mind continued to fascinate me and the writers I found most interesting were Wayne Dyer, Stuart Wilde, Depak Chopra, and Edgar Cayce. As my questions were answered, more appeared and I came to understand that we were only given what we could comprehend at any given time.

1984 was a hard year. My marriage was in trouble which led to health complications for my husband. His heart specialist referred him to a doctor at the University of Alberta. Dr. Hays was the Head of Psychiatry and wasn't an easy man to get to see so I was happy that my husband would have someone he could really talk to.

As it turned out he went twice but found it hard and didn't want to go any more. I had an intuition that I should try to get to see this man so I called my husband's heart specialist and explained that Tom no longer wanted to go but that I would like to meet him. The specialist arranged for me to see Dr. Hays and I was really grateful. I had been fascinated with the mind and human behavior for many years and here was an opportunity for me to see a prominent and respected man who specialized in those areas.

The first two visits were about my relationship and marriage. The third meeting changed everything because I had messages for him and told him things about himself that I could not possibly know. I continued to see him once a month for forty-five minutes for the next year and it was one of the most interesting and rewarding years of my life. He told me that I possessed a range of emotion that was beyond that of most people, he referred to it as, "The agony and Ecstasy." He told me that the degree to which I could feel joy and light was directly proportionate to the degree I could feel sorrow and darkness. He then told me that he had witnessed that joy and that if I was to experience the same degree of sorrow, it would be agony. He also told me that few people watched their thoughts much less file and retrieve them. We had some wonderful enlightening discussions about the human mind. At the last session, he told me to never let a doctor tell me I needed any type of medication for depression that the highs and lows were part of who I was and emotions were often picked up from outside sources. He also told me that it was a rewarding year for him as well but he couldn't keep billing Alberta Health when I wasn't really needing his help.

I missed those appointments and his sharp mind.

In February 1987 I had a hysterectomy that was supposed to put an end to my back pain. The back pain continued and got worse. I seldom took anything other than Advil for pain since I have a fear of any kind of drug. To deaden the pain I used to focus and send healing light to the painful area. One night as I was lying in bed and the pain was really bad, I suddenly found myself somewhere else. I was lying on a long, oval platform that was surrounded by beings with a human form but no features, just light. They were moving the platform into a huge tube that was filled with a brilliant light. The next thing I remembered was lying back in my bed and the pain was gone. In May I had a disc in my lower back rupture and that landed me in the hospital to have an emergency surgery. However, I have continued to have the same white light, tube experience on a random basis. I have come to believe these to be "check ups" and "treatments."

Towards the end of the 1980's on one of our trips to Hawaii with Bill and Darlene, I had the opportunity to spend several hours with my brother. He told me that there would be an opportunity for me coming up and to watch the newspapers . . . I would know it when I saw it. I read the papers religiously for the next few months and then one day saw an ad for a six week seminar with Val Van de Wal. I had met Val about five years earlier when Bill and Darlene took us to hear him speak. He scared the hell out of me at that time because I was not ready to hear what he was teaching and also because he was the only person, other than my brother, who had energy more powerful than my own. Val was a personal friend of Bill's as well as a business partner so we knew of him.

The first night of the six week seminar was free so that people could see what they were signing up for. It was not cheap and was very intensive so this was an opportunity to sample what was to come. Tom wasn't interested in the course but I signed up for it and as with Dr. Hays, it was a very enlightening experience.

By now I understood that nothing happened by accident and there were no coincidences. I had learned to interpret the communications I had with my guides and angels and there was never a day that went by that I didn't think of God. I was led to more and more books and found that I already knew what the authors were talking about. I understood that the universe was confirming to me what I knew and where I was on my path. Often these experiences would bring me to tears, to my knees, and to a place of deep humility. Anytime I speak of God or "feel" God, I cry. This has always been the case and I asked over and over why this was so.

One day in the early 2000's, I got my answer by way of a Buddhist calendar I kept by my kitchen sink. It was a page a day calendar and on this day it read, "In the spiritual life we must make a distinction between two kinds of loneliness. In the first, we are out of touch with God and look for someone or something that can give us a sense of belonging and happiness. In the second, the loneliness comes from an intimacy with God that is deeper and greater than our human senses can capture. We can think of this loneliness like blindness. The first comes from an absence of LIGHT and the second from too much LIGHT. The first we must try to outgrow with FAITH and HOPE. The second we must embrace in LOVE." The tears really flowed, my heart was exploding, and my inner light was really shining with this reading!!!

A few years later we were in Vancouver to visit my son, Shannon; his wife, Lesa; and son, Regan and were shopping in the downtown area where there are lots of homeless people. It caused me much pain to see these people and I asked God how I could help. The answer was immediate, "breathe in their pain and breathe back love . . .you can do this." As I was doing this exercise I found myself "detaching" from the homeless but loving more. I would later learn that this is an eastern philosophy that the Buddhists used but the western world does not understand it.

I would also come to understand that being detached didn't mean I didn't care. It is from this place of detachment that we are our most compassionate. We have learned who we are and we do not let other people's opinions of us define who we are. We ask for nothing from others and expect nothing from others. We become detached, very in tune to what is happening around us and very compassionate. We no longer have "baggage" taking up vital space within, we are free to serve however we are meant to.

During the same visit to Vancouver, I went with Shannon and his family to the Buddhist temple in Richmond. I knew it wasn't a coincidence that I just had the homeless experience so I paid close attention to what messages I was receiving in the temple. It was a very calming place to visit and I felt very at home. When we got back home I met with Bill and told him about the homeless experience and "breathe in pain, breathe out love." He told me this was from a past life in which I had been a Buddhist monk. As soon as he said this my entire body experienced a sensation like a mild electrical shock, validating the truth of what he said.

Both Wayne Dyer and Depak Chopra came to Edmonton during the 1990's and I made sure I got to see both of them. At each engagement I stood in line at the break along with my sister-in-law, Darlene, in order to get my program signed since I left my books at home. I got my autograph but also got a hug and words of encouragement from each of them which really, really surprised me. Darlene asked me why I rated a hug when no one else got one and I was asking the same question. I knew that they both "saw" me because of the words they spoke. They were like the psychics I'd been guided to see over the years. I have seen psychics since I was in my early twenties, although have never intentionally looked for one. They were also a way of confirming where I was on my path but I often wondered what they saw when they met me because without exception they have all said, "Oh my God" and some have refused to take any payment.

I got my answer to my question when Darlene and I took some courses through the University of Alberta's Department of Extension in 2001. One of the courses we took was called Kirlian Photography. The instructor took a photo of our hands and when the photos developed we could see the shapes of our hands and four circle-like shapes on each of our fingers. How the circles were shaped, whether they were broken or not, and the shade meant something.

For the second picture, she asked us to think of God as she took the picture. When they were developed, she gave each of us our picture along with an interpretation of the meaning. My photo showed no shape of a hand at all, it was just a bright white mass with a purple and blue shade of colour outlining the light. She explained that it indicated a very powerful connection to God and that she had never seen a photo like it before. She asked if I channelled information and I told her that I did and that I was constantly getting messages of some sort. She then told me that I was a mystic and asked if I knew what that meant. When I told her no, she explained that a mystic was someone who saw God everywhere and in everything. A mystic had a clear channel to the Divine and this channel allowed the Divine to work through the person. As soon as she told me this my entire body once again felt an energy like an electrical shock . . . the same experience I had when Bill told me of my past life as a Buddhist monk.

In the late 1990's, we made a summer trip to Sedona, Arizona. In previous months I had come across ads for Sedona in every newspaper I picked up. I told Tom that it was important that I go there, so we made that our summer holiday and drove. It was a great experience driving through Utah, Montana, and Idaho but it was a fantastic experience driving through Arizona. I knew the moment we crossed the border. When Tom asked me how I knew, I showed him my arms which were covered with bumps and all the hair was standing straight up. On the inside I could feel and "see" my light getting brighter and brighter and could feel a vibration from my toes to my crown chakra (located on the top of my head). I couldn't contain my tears and when Tom asked why I was crying I had no answer. I just felt overcome with emotions . . . very, very happy emotions.

We stayed in Sedona for ten days and really enjoyed it. I had done some research, so I knew that there was an energy vortex in the area which attracted a lot of "New Age" people along with a lot of movie people who had purchased huge expensive homes. One day we wondered into a shop that sold crystals, gems, and rocks. It had a very calming feel to it and we took our time looking at the different stones trying to decided which one I was going to buy. I finally decided on a piece of amethyst for myself and a piece of rose quartz for my sister-in-law, Darlene.

As we were paying, the lady behind the counter told me she had been waiting for me. I must have looked puzzled because she then said she was a psychic and knew she would be meeting a stranger with many questions and that I was the stranger. Tom must have looked skeptical because she looked at him and said you have a son and daughter at home by themselves but you don't need to worry about them they are fine. I made an appointment to see her the next day and then I found out that she was also a licensed hypnotherapist.

The next day when I went to see her, I told her that she should choose what would serve me best; a psychic reading or hypnosis. She looked at me for a few minutes then told me that hypnosis was the way to go. She had me sit in a chair and relax. As she talked to me she suggested that I climb a set of stairs and when I finally get to the top I would meet the person I was supposed to meet and we would have a conversation. That person would have the answers to my questions. I remember very little of this experience. I remember getting to the top of the stairs and seeing someone waiting for me. The next thing I knew I was sitting in the chair and she was calling my name, telling me I must come back. She told me later that she had a very hard time bringing me back to the present and told me that I called the person that I met by name and the name was Jesus. I have no knowledge of the conversation I had with that person but I felt different.

One day we wondered into a shopping area where there was an ice cream shop so we decided to get an ice cream. I found the music that was playing very interesting and when we finally got to the counter to make our selection the music changed. As soon as this happened, I felt extremely homesick and started to cry. The music had a hum in the background and a vibration that was the same as my mom's washing machine and I felt like a little girl again.

Since I wore contacts in those days, I told my husband that one was bothering me and I went to the washroom. After I got myself under control, I went back to get my ice cream but knew I would have to find out the name of the song in order to find out why I felt as I did. The next day I had some time to myself and I went back to the ice cream shop to get the name of the music if possible. The same fellow was behind the counter and he remembered me very well. He also remembered that the music seemed to affect me so he was not surprised when I asked about it. He found the cassette that had been playing and showed it to me but told me that he bought it in Phoenix, not in Sedona. As I was writing down the title he told me that since the music had made such an impression on me I should take his copy. When I tried to pay him for it, he refused the money and told me it was his way of helping me on my path. I would later find out that the selection that affected me so much every time I heard it was called, "Light Years from Home. "The 1990'S came to an end with my mom's life also coming to an end. She passed away Nov 28, 1999 the morning of her and dad's Fiftieth Anniversary. I turned fifty on February 24, 2000 and my dad passed away in March, 2000. The new millennium was beginning as "endings" in my life continued. My marriage was coming to an end as well although neither myself or my husband wanted to take the first step. We were both unhappy but ending a thirty-four year marriage was incredibly hard. We didn't want to hurt the other even though we were both already hurting. How do you walk away from someone you love but have outgrown? On September 3, 2003 I left the home I'd known for twenty-three years and the man I'd loved since I was fifteen. It was the hardest thing I have ever done and know on some level it tore my husband apart as well. Sometimes it takes more than love to hold a marriage together.

I had managed to rent a basement suite in a home owned by a fellow woman Realtor that I liked and respected. When I enquired about the suite she assumed it was for clients and when I told her it was for me she was shocked. I swore her to secrecy so word wouldn't get around the Realtor community; they would find out soon enough. I told no one in the office what I was going through but they all knew something wasn't right. I am a very outgoing and communicative person but that was not the person they saw any more. It was a very dark place I found myself in and I wasn't eating or sleeping, so I knew I needed to talk to someone.

I called my doctor at the end of the week and when she saw me, she was shocked. She had been my doctor for many years so she was very concerned since she had never seen me like this before. She told me that I was going to have to take something to help me sleep. She gave me a prescription for two weeks of sleeping pills but told me to take half a pill at supper to start because they were strong and I had never taken sleeping pills before. That Friday night I took the half-a-pill with some supper.

I had just finished eating when my old neighbor called me (she had gotten the number from my husband). She and her husband had lived beside us for many years and we spent a lot of time together, so they knew us very well. She told me that she was keeping an eye on Tom since I had always done the cooking and she wanted me to know that he was okay. He seemed to be doing fine because he was smiling and using the barbecue every night. I don't remember ending the conversation I just remember the intense pain and the darkness. Dr. Hay's words came back to me and I remembered his telling me that if I ever hit the sorrow and darkness it would be agony. I don't remember taking the rest of the pills, nor do I remember my neighbor calling back. She would tell me months later that she was very uncomfortable when I ended the conversation with her and told her husband that something was wrong but didn't know what it was.

A few hours later she decided to call back and I have no memory of answering the phone nor our conversation. She asked what I was doing and I told her that I was just waiting for mom and dad who were coming to take me home. She said she started to panic because she knew my parents had passed away. She told her husband and they called Tom. They had no way of getting into my suite so they had to get my landlady to let them in.

Between them they got me into the car and to the hospital. I woke up the next afternoon to a doctor with a grave expression standing over me. He told me that I was fortunate to be waking up but all I could think of was my mom. The memory of seeing my mom came back and I started crying. I don't remember much of that night but I remember vividly the intense white light and the incredible feelings of peace, freedom, and love. It was like being in a tunnel that was filled with mist and white light and then my mom was walking towards me. She looked exactly like she did before she hurt her hip and was smiling. When she reached me, she hugged me, it felt so wonderful, and I felt so happy. My mom was a big woman and when she hugged, you knew it. The hug felt the same, she smelled the same, and the love I felt from her was washing over me like waves. She said something to me but I don't remember what it was. She hugged me again and then started to back away . I tried to follow her but it was like an invisible wall between us. I couldn't touch her anymore and as she backed away, she began to fade into the mist. I wanted to go with her so badly and I called and called but she was gone.

All of these memories were coming back to me as the doctor was leaning over me and checking my eyes. I felt a coldness and darkness settle over me and knew I would not see my mom or dad for a very long time. After the doctor left, another one came in and spoke to me for awhile. I remember nothing of what he said or what I said. I found out that I was released with the understanding that I would continue to see the second doctor who turned out to be a psychiatrist. I remember Tom showing up to take me home and telling me he had called Bill. Bill told him to take me to his place. I remember sitting in the family room at Bill's and his asking me if I saw mom. I told him I'd seen her but she didn't want me. Bill told me that it wasn't that she didn't want me, it was not my time to be with her. He said that mom had a message for me and this was the only way I was to receive it. It couldn't come through my angels or through him.

The next few months were the darkest of my entire life

and I struggled every day with not wanting to be here. I had felt the presence of God my entire life. I always felt the light within me and had always known there were angels around me, guiding and guarding me. Now I felt nothing but darkness. It was terrifying and I have never felt more alone in my entire life. Somewhere deep inside I knew that God would never abandon me and this thought is what I hung onto. I prayed all the time for the darkness to leave me but it didn't.

Looking back on that year, I can see I was being taken care of. It was the busiest year I ever had in real estate and the clients just seemed to show up. I was kept very busy. Some of the clients that showed up had been through marriage breakups so they understood what I was going through. I had clients and Realtors calling me at night to see if I was okay and I was at my office during the day. I can say that it was the Realtors in my office, some other offices in Sherwood Park, and those special clients that helped me through that first six months. I prayed every day and knew God and my angels were with me even though I never felt them.

At the beginning of December I started getting stressed about Christmas. I didn't want to be around anyone including my family but I didn't know how I was going to manage it. One morning I woke up and immediately thought of Mexico. It wasn't much, just a thought. No lights, no sensations anywhere on my body, no connections to anything else but I was really excited. I had NO contact from the astral plane in any way, shape, or form for several months; only darkness. I said Mexico to myself over and over but nothing, not even the mildest intuition.

I finally decided that I would have to take a leap of faith so I called Bill and told him I wanted to go to Mexico for

Christmas. I told him what happened (and what didn't). He suggested a new travel company called The Flight Centre and gave me an address.

I went there and met an agent and told him I wanted to spend Christmas and New Year's in Mexico but didn't know where. I had no intuitions about this young man nor anything guiding me, so I told him I didn't care where. I just needed a nice beach, warm water, and a safe hotel because I was alone. I asked him where he'd been in Mexico that he liked. He thought for a few minutes and then suggested a resort in the Mayan Riviera. It was a large complex close to a small town and huge marina . . .very safe and a nice beach. I booked it and left.

I was feeling afraid because I knew my kids wouldn't be happy with this decision and because I really didn't know what the hell I was doing. I asked Ev, my friend and co-worker, to look after my business while I was gone.; She was concerned about my going but understood why I needed to. By now the office knew I had left my husband but nothing else. I told no one about the pills and I never did until a couple of years ago. I assumed my husband told the kids but I never discussed the situation with anyone. My kids understood why I wanted to go and I promised to call on Christmas Day.

I felt very sure of myself when I flew out of Edmonton but when I deplaned into a small airport and had to walk across the runway into the building, I had a panic attack. An older couple helped me into the building and sat me down. I assured them that I was fine, just my first time away by myself. They stuck with me until we got through customs and out to the bus that I needed to take to the resort. They were going in the opposite direction so I thanked them and got on my bus.

It was dark by this time even though it was only around 7:30p.m.. The trip from Cancun to the resort was forty-five minutes and was an eye opener. As soon as the bus left the airport, the tour guide yelled, "Who wants a Corona." It was an interesting and loud trip to the resort. The resort itself was very impressive and I felt more secure as I checked in. I noticed an older lady and two men standing together not far from the desk. I must have looked tired and confused because the lady came forward, asking what room I was in. When I told her, she pointed me in the right direction and suggested I unpack and join them since they were Canadian and I sounded like I was as well.

I unpacked and went back out to the foyer where they were waiting for me. I introduced myself and told them where I was from. They did the same and I found out they were from Vancouver. We went to the restaurant so I could get something to eat. The lady asked why my husband wasn't with me (still had my rings on) and I explained that I had left a thirty-four year marriage and needed some time alone to do some healing.

The three of them looked at each other and then she said, "you'll be in good hands, my husband and I are both psychiatrists retired from U.B.C." The single fellow said he was a retired professor from the University of Alberta in Edmonton and his wife was back in their room because she had a cold.

I was stunned and started to cry explaining that I was a spiritual person but had been out of touch with my angels for a long time. I had been praying this trip would help me. I got a huge hug from all of them and they said they had another week left and would be there for me the whole time. It was an amazing week and although I still could feel no contact with the spirit world, I knew the spirits were with me.

The morning my new friends left, I got their addresses and phone numbers. We promised to keep in touch which we did for several years. I would met them for coffee whenever I went to Vancouver. I kept a picture of the four of them on my nightstand for a long time.

After they left, I went for lunch and was eating when a young couple stopped at my table asking if they could join me. There were other tables available but I said "sure." They introduced themselves and said they'd noticed me with two couples so I told them the others had gone home and I was there for another week on my own. The lady said that I was always sad looking even though I appeared to be having a good time. Once again I explained why I was by myself. They looked at each other and then smiled at me. He said that he was a minister in Salt Lake City. His wife laughed and said to her husband, "I guess we found out who the book was for." I must have looked puzzled as the wife explained that she packed a certain book to take with them because she knew they would meet someone who needed it.

Once again the tears and my explanation of being a spiritual person but without my constant spirit companions was told. They both took one of my hands and he told me that my angels were with me and I would feel their presence once I got through the dark time. He then told me that I was here to do God's work and that the separation was part of the plan. They were leaving the next morning but I got the book from her before they left. I've read and re-read it and has been a source of comfort for me. The title of that book is, The Prayer of Jabez.

One night after they left, I was having supper and a lady a little older than myself asked if I was eating alone. I told her I was and she asked if she could join me. I found out that her name was Manon, she was French from Montreal, and this was her first Christmas alone. Her husband had passed away in the spring. We had a great conversation, found out we were both spiritual, and had very similar beliefs. She had only two days left and we took a tour together the next day.

On the tour, she told me all about her Welsh husband who had come to Montreal twenty-five years earlier. They met and were married shortly after and had a wonderful marriage but no children. She said her husband was very spiritual having old customs and beliefs that he brought from Wales. They went back many times and she said she'd never been in a more spiritual place than Wales. When he was dying he told her that he would be back as a butterfly and would always be with her. The day after the funeral, she was sitting on her balcony when a black butterfly landed on her arm. She said she knew immediately that it was George, her departed husband.

The tour we took was to Tulum and it was hot that day. We walked all through the ruins and just sat down to rest when she started to laugh. I looked at her, she pointed to her leg, and there was a big, black butterfly. She reached her hand out and the butterfly left her leg for her finger. It was such a beautiful moment and I knew my angels were showing me that they were still with me. Manon left the next morning and I ended up with only two days left. On my second last day I went to the ruins at Chitchen Itza. It was here on top of the pyramid that I felt my angels for the first time in many months and knew everything was going to be alright.

2004

In May of 2004, I woke up with words running through my head. I needed to record them so I found a pen and paper and started writing. When the words ended I went back and read what I had written and was stunned. Stunned by the words, also by the fact that my angels were communicating again but in the form of a poem. This would be the first of twenty poems that came to me over a three year period. They were guideposts for me on the long road back to ME however that ME was no longer.

THE STRUGGLE

You cannot go home
My messenger said
Until HE calls for you
But I am so very tired said I
Feeling HIS messages
Not getting thru
You have a lot of work to do
She then said to me
The windows will open
And LIGHT will shine
The path to follow
You will then see
I have chosen to live in LIGHT
And send LOVE to all I know
And trust that they in turn will LOVE

And the circle of LIGHT will grow
We were given free will
And the choice is yours to make
But freedom gives us many paths
Now which one do you take
If you quiet your noisy head
And listen with your heart
If you trust the faint whispers you hear
You and TRUTH will never be far apart

That afternoon my friend and fellow Realtor dragged me to a complex of duplexes under construction. She told me I needed to get out of the basement and buy my own home. I suspected that I was the topic of conversation in my office and Ev was "voted" to get me back to the land of the living. I ended up buying a half-duplex that would be completed mid-July. With the help of my family, I moved into my new home. On the day I was moving more words came to me and I had to find a pen. I recorded them on one of the moving boxes. Like the first one it was very much my life and a beautiful message.

STARTING OVER

My children have families
Of their own
My mother and father have both
Gone home.
My husband has chosen
A path alone
I am now free
To be me
Not the me they thought
I should be
But the me deep inside
I am starting to see
Indeed it is
She

Earlier that year a Realtor in my office had convinced me to go to the Royal Lepage Annual Conference being held in Quebec City in September. Don and I have a really good connection and I remember the first time I met him. When I shook his hand the thought came to me immediately, "So we meet again." I had a very strong feeling we had a past life together but it would be fifteen years before he and I would have a discussion about this. I have had several messages for him since that time. I decided that if I was going to the convention I would take an extra week and go to Montreal to see Manon. On the flight to Quebec City, I had more words show up and they were recorded on a napkin. As before the poem spoke of my life.

CHANGES

The sands shift
Once a valley
Now a hill
The landscape of life
Never ending metamorphosis
The only constant
Perpetual
Shifting

After this poem I spent a good deal of time thinking about where they came from and came to believe that my guides and angels were communicating with me in the poems.

I stayed in Quebec City for a week. The conference was held in a building inside the old walled city. When I had time to myself, I spent it going through the very old restored buildings. The old city is a World Heritage Site so it was a fantastic place to explore. The whole time I was inside the walled city, I had very powerful intuitions of being there before. In some of the old buildings the feelings were so strong that I had glimpses of myself in another time.

One of the planned events we could pay for was a dinner cruise on the St. Lawrence and I wanted this experience. I was wandering around the top deck when an older woman approached me, asked my name, and what branch I was with. When she found out I was alone, she suggested I join her office which was an all-woman-office from Toronto. She told me I would have fun as they were a bunch of "wild" women. She also told me that one of the Realtors was a very good psychic. We went down to the lower deck to find the women and when we did, she introduced me, told them I was alone, and that she'd invited me to join them.

A tall woman with long, red hair stood up and approached us. The lady I was standing with asked her what she saw for me. I assumed with that question that the red head was the psychic but I was not prepared for what she said. She held her hand up and asked me to stop and stand still which I did. She then proceeded with "ladies you are looking at a powerful woman but she doesn't know it yet. She is a mystic and now she has clouds over her head and chains on her ankles but when she's free nothing will stop her. She is here as a teacher and gets her words from the angels."

I was stunned and embarrassed but all the women welcomed me. They were indeed "wild" women and I had more fun than I'd had in many, many years. When my week was up I took the train to Montreal. I had a great time because Manon took time every day to show me her city.

We had some fabulous meals in the different ethnic areas. I didn't have the same feelings that I had in Quebec City but I enjoyed my time spent there as well.

2005

April 2005 brought me more words, these appearing on an early morning walk headed into a stunning sunrise. By now I was never without pen and paper. These words touched me deeply and brought forth tears. I found that when words were coming to me, I had a tingling in my crown chakra, a feeling of humbleness and that I was loved. I was feeling the connection to GOD and angels way more that I had in the past and while it was beautiful I was wondering where it all would lead.

LYNN'S SONG

Ahhh she said
As she gazed upon the sun
She felt the warm rays cradle her
And then they were as one
Ahhh she said
As she felt the gentle breeze
Caress her skin so lovingly
As raindrops touching leaves
Ahhh she said
As the instruments played to her soul
And washed away all loneliness
The music made her whole
Ahhh she said
As the colours wrapped her tight

And guided her so gently
Towards the waiting light
Ahhh she said
As she gazed into HIS eyes
For then she knew
Her path was realized

In March 2005, a single woman I worked with told me it was time to start living my life again and time to meet new people. She took me to my first single's dance where I was danced off my feet, but I felt really uncomfortable and couldn't wait to go home. I started to go to this particular place every Friday night and eventually enjoyed myself and the people I met. On Saturday nights I started to go to a different single's club, the music and people were a different crowd although some were the same.

In April I was introduced to a fellow by the name of Gilbert and we really connected. We became really good friends and had a lot of fun together. He was also very spiritual so we had much in common besides music and dancing. He convinced me to go to an event called "Reaching Out." It was an organization that held meetings every second Wednesday in a church basement for people who were single through no choice of their own.

His cousin was running the group but wanted to leave as the coordinator but couldn't until she could find someone to take over. Gilbert thought I would be perfect for the role. The leader was responsible for booking speakers for the meetings. The organization got funding from the government so it had some excellent speakers. My fellow co-worker who introduced me to dancing also went to "Reaching Out" so I knew a couple of people. I went to several of the meetings to see if this was something I was interested in doing. It was a big commitment twice a month and in downtown Edmonton. After much discussion with Gilbert, I finally agreed to take it over but not until the end of August.

One evening in June I was driving home from helping Gilbert renovate his kitchen, when the next poem appeared. I pulled over so I could write the words down and when I went back and read them I was again moved and filled with questions. Where did these poems come from? Why was I getting them? What did this mean? I often thought of what the psychic in Toronto said that I was here to teach and my words would come from the angels.

BELIEVE

When you gaze upon a bird
With its wings outspread
You know that it can fly

You think you understand the Truth
So never ask the why
You see my friend that simple bird
Flies because it knows it can
What would the world be like my friend
If that thought took root in man
If we trusted where we came from
And believed that love
Is what we are
Then love would fill the universe
To the furthest reaching star

I was finding it hard to understand what was happening in my life and because I was constantly asking "why?" my brother Bill sometimes became frustrated with me. During one of our meetings he told me that I believed but I didn't "BELIEVE" and he asked, "how many burning bushes do you need to see before you just accept and BELIEVE?" He has always referred to me as a "spiritual councilor" but I see myself as a "messenger" and this feels right to me. I knew that I was in my own way and needed to find a way around the part of me that always needed to know.

In June my world would be rocked even more than it had been in the previous year. In the first week of June I had a series of very graphic visions that shook me and left me questioning my sanity. On the morning of Friday June tenth, in that space of time just before fully awakening, my mind was filled with a golden light. This was not uncommon for me and I came to associate this with a shift in awareness preceding more knowledge coming to me. Usually as the light faded I would wake up, always with a sense of peace.

This morning; however, was far, far different. As the

light faded a very, very disturbing vision appeared. I saw hands and feet with nails through them. The details were alarming. There was black hair on the part of the arms and legs that I saw, drops of blood landed on dirt, and dust formed as the blood landed. I could smell blood and dust but heard nothing. Both hands had the palms with nails in them facing me and the feet had one foot over the other with a nail through the top of the foot. The hands were above the feet. No body, nothing but the hands, feet, and the dripping blood. I was terrified but couldn't wake up or get the vision out of my mind as it seemed to go on and on. I could hear myself saying over and over, "I accept Jesus Christ." While I was saying this I felt a brilliant, white light behind my right eye and the right side of my head started vibrating. Gradually the vision disappeared and I woke up. I was ice cold, crying, and had trouble breathing. The room was so cold I could see my breath.

I got out of bed, got the phone, and called Bill. I couldn't talk straight and couldn't stop shaking. Bill finally shouted at me to "calm down" and as I started to settle, I was able to tell him about the vision. He talked to me for awhile and then told me that there would be more visions before whatever was happening ended. I spent a long time in the tub before I finally started to warm up. I knew I was in no condition to drive, so I stayed home and spent much of my time outside walking. I felt like I was only partly present with the other part of me somewhere else, as if in a dream. Bill called to see if I was okay and said they'd come to see me on Saturday.

On Saturday I spent time talking with Bill and gradually began to feel like myself again. I knew I was going through a spiritual shift from the messages I had been receiving but

I had no idea what was to come.

Tuesday I had an appointment to show some condos to a client and as we were passing from one room to another, I had another vision. This time I saw myself in a long, brown garment; kneeling on a dirt floor; washing a man's feet in an earthenware bowl. The emotions I felt were of intense love, compassion, and humbleness. As the vision passed, I found my client shaking me, asking if I was okay and why was the room suddenly so cold. I told her I wasn't feeling well and also found the room cold. There was no way to explain what happened, so I just suggested we finish looking at the condo and then I would take her home. She would later refer to that condo as the "spooky one."

I called Bill that night to tell him about the second vision and found myself much calmer (and warmer). I agreed to meet Gilbert and his cousin at "Reaching Out" on Wednesday night because he felt I could help her with some of the problems that she was experiencing. When I got to the top of the hill that leads into the river valley going into downtown, I had another vision. It was of myself dressed again in the long, brown garment; walking down a hill on a dirt path. I was filled with love and an euphoric happiness. It was gone in seconds but it did scare me because I was driving. I found I was cold and the car interior was cold enough to see my breath but I felt fantastic.

As I entered the church basement where "Reaching Out" was held, I saw Gilbert and a woman. He came over and asked me what happened to me saying, "you are glowing." I noticed other people starting at me also so I went to the bathroom to have a look at myself. I did have a happy look; like the glow of a bride on her wedding day. I sat with Gilbert and his cousin to listen to the speaker and then spent time talking to the cousin and making plans to meet with her in the next week or two. I was introduced to people as the person who would be taking over "Reaching Out" meetings starting in August. Gilbert introduced me to the people he knew, and the woman I would be taking over from introduced me to others. I had a few, "you sure look like a happy lady" comments as I met people and later I said to Gilbert, "they probably wonder what I'm taking or smoking."

I told Gilbert that I wasn't ready to talk about what was going on with me but I would share with him when I was ready. By the time I got home that night, it was too late to call Bill and bring him up to date on the latest vision. Thursday morning I got up early to go for a long walk. I headed east towards a beautiful sunrise and had only gone a few blocks when I had yet another vision of myself in the familiar brown garment. This time climbing up the hill on a dusty path but instead of the ecstasy I felt the previous night, I was feeling a lot of pain, absolute agony.

When the vision cleared, I was standing on the sidewalk, crying, a man with his dog was walking towards me. He was very concerned and asked if he could help. I just told him that I'd received some bad news and was having trouble dealing with it. He wanted to walk me home but I told him I needed to go for a long walk. By now I was feeling like I was coming apart, I didn't understand what was happening, and I was afraid of what the next days would bring.

I called Bill that night and told him about the last two visions and we agreed to meet for coffee on Saturday. Friday evening, one week from the first vision, I had an experience that shook me up even more than the visions. I finished supper and was cleaning up the kitchen when

I had a very physical experience. For me to explain the experience, you need to understand that the human body has energy meridians called chakras running through it. There are seven main chakras that run up our spine starting at the base (the root chakra) all the way to the top of our head (the crown chakra). There was an "energy" that started at my root chakra and ran up to my crown *chakra*, down the outside of my body, and back up again through my chakras. It was very intense and the only way I can describe it would be to say it was like having orgasms over and over.

Now some of you may be thinking WOW that would be great but it wasn't great. It became more and more intense almost to the threshold of pain and wouldn't stop. I couldn't even walk. I kept asking my angels what was happening to me and all I got was the word *kundalini* over and over. I had heard the word and knew it had something to do with East Indian yogis but couldn't understand what the hell it had to do with me. This experience lasted for over a minute which seemed like forever. The only reason it stopped was because I started to chant the word "Ave." I had no idea why but I just kept chanting the one word over and over in a certain range of tones.

The energy stopped and I was standing in my kitchen chanting "Ave" with tears running down my face. I finally stopped chanting and just collapsed on my floor in tears. It is impossible to describe what I felt like . . . like "I" was melting away and another "I" was replacing me. I had no idea why any of this happened or what it meant. I had no one I could turn to except my brother, Bill, and it seemed to me like my angels and guides left me to fend for myself.

That night I had a stiff drink of brandy before I went to bed and thought to myself, I'm either going to be in an institute or I'm going to be a drunk. I met Bill and Darlene for coffee on Saturday and told them what happened since Thursday. We had a long conversation. Bill then told me that the visions were finished but he couldn't help me anymore and that I needed to see a minister.

The next day my sister-in-law, Mary, called to tell me that someone from my home town had passed away and the funeral would be the following week. I asked who was doing the service and found out it was the same lady minister who had done both my mom and dad's services. I asked Mary to make an appointment for me to talk to Lois after the service and told her that I would explain later.

I went to Chapters Bookstore in search of a book to explain what *kundalini* meant and was led right to the book. When I took it off the shelf, I could feel an energy from it. This was not unfamiliar to me but what was new was the heat that came with the energy. Over the next few days I read through the book, not page for page, just wherever I happened to open it. I have read certain books this way for many years. Since I was in search of specific answers, I knew I would be guided to the pages I needed to read. I found out that *kundalini* is the spiritual force that lies dormant in every human being. It lays at the base of the spine and once awakened rises up the spine and finds expression in the forms of spiritual knowledge, mystical vision, psychic powers; and ultimately, enlightenment. Usually this is a state attained only by advanced meditation and yoga. Since I didn't meditate or do yoga, I assumed that this came to me because I always received messages, had visions, and knew things I had no way of knowing.

A few days later I drove to my hometown for the funeral service of someone from my past who had meant something to me. After the service I met with Lois and explained in detail what transpired over the past week. She asked me what I knew of the Bible and I told her I had never read it. She told me what she thought my experiences meant but asked me to meet with someone in the city who was much more knowledgeable about my experiences. She gave me the name and number of a United Church minister and told me that she would call to let him know about me.

I called in the next few days and went to see Rev. C the following Sunday. We had a long conversation about my life in the past few years and then I told him about the visions and other experiences. He also asked me what I knew of the Bible and when I told him "nothing," he smiled and said, "I thought as much." He then proceeded to tell me that I had experienced the Crucifixion and Resurrection, although not in sequence. I told him that I found a book entitled *Kundalini* and told him what it meant. He said it made sense in light of all the other experiences. He told me that the word "Ave" was in fact calling God and that I had been born to serve. However getting married, having children and a career, had taken me away from what I came to do. Now that I was free, on my own and the children were raised with lives of their own, I was being called to service.

When he told me this I couldn't stop crying and showed him the second poem that had come to me "Starting Over." He hugged me and said, "my dear you are a mystic." I told him that Dr. Hays had called me the same thing in 1985 but I would like his interpretation of what a "mystic" was. He told me that a mystic was a person who sees God everywhere and in everything. They have a channel through which God can work and are here for the purpose of serving God, however they are directed to do. I laughed and told him it seemed we had the same boss. He told me that the spiritual path was not an easy one but was rewarding. I asked if he believed that the closer we got to the Light, the greater the threat to the Darkness we became, and he agreed. This was a comfort for me because I was feeling like I needed to protect myself more and more from a dark energy.

In July of 2005, I took my grandson, Kieran, to Vancouver to visit my son, Shannon, his wife, Lesa, and his son, Regan. It was a wonderful trip and I had two poems show up while we were there. The first one appeared when I took the boys to a place called Deep Cove on the ocean and was watching them skip rocks. When I went back and read what I had written, I saw both Kieran and Regan in the words.

THE WARRIOR PRINCE

His name means Dark Prince
But oft is misunderstood

For its darkness that he chases
From the many paths of good
He has a deepness to his soul
Many times he has seen this world
And many times fought battles
To witness Light uncurled
Seems only in the darkest times
It is to the Light we reach
But in the Light is the way to live
And that he is here to teach
His struggles will be many
But guided he will be
And when you live your life in Light
It is a different world you see
Rich or poor will matter not
He will fight for justice for all
He will have a vision to follow
And he will walk proud and tall

A few days later I took the boys for a walk on the sea wall and the second poem came to me. This was much longer than the others and when I went back and read what I'd written, I was again in tears. This was about me, what I'd been through, and about the help I'd gotten from Bill. Sitting on a bench looking at the ocean, I had a deep sense of peace come over me and knew my angels were with me. I also knew that I was being healed by these poems coming to me from beyond.

WINGS

There was a little robin
Who somehow lost her way
No matter where her wings had taken her
It seemed she could not stay
There was a longing deep inside
For what she did not know
She couldn't fly beyond the clouds
To where the sun would show
That even though her world seemed gray
And beauty did not shine
The world in fact was filled with love
And bright light so divine
That when she finally did break thru
The clouds and into light
She felt a deep assurance

Everything would be alright
Her red breast gently swelled
Beneath the warm rays of the sun
She spread her wings to test her strength
And flew, a new day had begun
She felt a purpose
And a new path she was shown
Looking back from where she now flew
She could see how much she'd grown
She had a whole world waiting
And hurts she could help mend
And none of this would have happened
Without one special friend
He had listened quietly to her
Every story he had heard
And he had guided her through ageless wisdom
Now she says thanks to Thunderbird

This poem was the first one to be published by The Poetry Institute of Canada in 2008.

In August 2005, I took over "Reaching Out." I touched and was touched by the people who came to listen to the speakers that were booked for the remainder of the year. The meetings were two Wednesdays a month and consisted of a speaker, followed by a social get-together. I made a point of baking four dozen cookies for every meeting which proved to be work for me but much appreciated by those that came to the meetings. In late August, I went with Gilbert's cousin to a sweat lodge and found the experience very spiritual. Within a few hours of the experience, I had another poem arrive which was very strong and touched me deeply.

MAN OR GOD

What did I see in my souls eye
That led me to this place
Am I here or far beyond
The masses of this race
While I am here in flesh and blood
As is plain to see
My soul remembers other times
And its there I sometimes long to be
Once the wise ones of the lands
Knew of plants and herbs to heal
Now these are seen as weeds and killed
And chemicals seen as real
Women earning the right to vote
Was a celebration to behold

But still in some lands girls are aborted
And the darkness makes me cold
Lands that once bore prophets
Now bear terrorists, hate and fear
As children are dying of starvation or aids
"Where is god" now is the cry I hear
It is not the creator who destroys this world
It is the hand of man
It is greed and hate and fear
And hiding from truth whenever we can
Seems only in the darkest times
It is to the light we reach
But in light is the only way to live
As prophets have been sent to teach
As my time here now
Is drawing to an end
I can only watch and pray
And Love and Light I'll send and send

I found the poem related to my past lives. When I read and reread it, I felt a power coming from the words along with a strong sense of purpose. The poem spoke of being "beyond" the masses and this really resonated with my entire being. I had always known that I was an old soul and more evolved that most people. After reading that statement some of you will have formed an opinion that I am arrogant and have a big ego. This is not true, I simply am what I am. Our judgment of others does not define them, nor does it hurt them; however, it does define us and impedes our growth. Judgment of others slows our growth more than anything and if left unchecked leads to much damage to our inner being.

Several months after the poem came to me, I was loaning a book to a friend and found the first four lines of this poem, I had written them in 1979. By now I'd had so many unexplainable experiences that I just accepted and questioned less. I was still a frustration for Bill because I continued to look for answers where there were none.

Towards the end of 2005, there was an excellent speaker at "Reaching Out" who was a psychologist. We hit it off and met for coffee several times in the following weeks. I found myself telling her about taking the pills and seeing a certain psychiatrist for a year. I told her how the first few months seemed normal to me but then he would take his shoes off, prop his feet on his desk, lean back, and start talking to me about himself. I told her that I asked at the end of 2004, if I still needed to see him. He had told me that I didn't need to come back and that it was him who needed me not me that needed him.

She asked if his office advised me off his death over Christmas and I told her they called in March 2005. When I asked her why she asked me that question, she told me that he committed suicide in his office over Christmas. I could just feel the cold roll over me. She reached for my hand and told me that he found someone to talk to in me, but there was nothing I could have done to change his mind. I felt such compassion for this man because I had been in that dark place and but for the Grace of God I would be gone as well.

In October, Don (from my office) went back to Turkey. He had been there during the summer, loved the area, and decided to purchase a condo there. When he got back from his trip he came to my office, told me what he bought, and that I could use it any time I wanted. Without even thinking I said, "next September, the whole month." I really surprised myself but just talking about Turkey and hearing about Don's adventures awaken a feeling that I really needed to visit this country.

The next time that I talked to my friend, Treva, I told her that I was going to Turkey in September 2006 and as I did, she replied immediately that she was coming with me. It was almost a year away but we were both excited about this trip and both felt that it was something we had to do.

2006

006 found me enjoying my Friday and Saturday nights dancing and also enjoying the people I had met. I have always loved music, dancing, and color; for me the three went together. Music would make me want to dance and dancing in my mind meant color. This explains why I love to travel to places like Mexico, Cuba, and Turkey. They are all "emotional" cultures which means they are passionate and their lives are filled with color, music, and dancing.

On the first weekend after New Year's, I woke up knowing I needed to go dancing that night and so did a friend who sometimes came with me. I called her, told her we were going dancing that night and would both meet interesting men. We got to the club and found a table just before the music started. As I sat down, I could feel energy from behind me. I turned around to see if I knew anyone at that table but I didn't. However, I knew the energy was coming from a man with his back to me. As soon as the music started, I was asked to dance but when I sat down again I decided that I would ask the stranger to dance.

He seemed surprised that I would ask, so I told him I came to dance and he looked like a good dancer. As soon as his arm went around me, I could feel his anger and questioned whether he was the one I was to meet. As soon as I did, the name Luzia came to me and I wondered what the connection was and who she was. He was a good dancer and I enjoyed dancing with him but not his energy. When the set was finished, we went back to the tables and as I sat down was asked to dance again. It was a few sets later before I sat out a few dances and was able to process this fellow behind me.

I had no intuitions about anyone else I danced with nor did I feel any energy from any other table. While I was sifting through my feelings, he came back and asked me to dance and this time we exchanged names. I found out his was Tony and he worked at the refineries. I could still feel the anger but I was sure that he was who I was meant to meet. We ended up dancing together quite a lot and I enjoyed dancing with him. As the dance was coming to an end he asked me to go for coffee and I explained I had a friend riding with me but I would be back the next Saturday and would see him if he was there. My friend also met a very nice person who also asked for her phone number, so the evening ended on a high note!

The following weekend I met Tony at the dance and we spent most of the evening dancing together. I agreed to go for coffee later and met him at a twenty-four hour Tim Horton's close by. As we sat down with our coffee, I could feel his anger and stress and wasn't surprised to see he had tears in his eyes. When I told him I was a good listener and it seemed like he needed to talk, he started to cry. He was upset with himself and said he had no idea what was going on because he never cried and certainly never talked to someone he just met. He told me that he had a funny feeling as soon as he met me that he could and should talk to me which was why he asked me out for coffee.

I found out that he was Portuguese and he and his wife, Luzia, came to Canada in the early 1980s. He was a year older than I was and Luzia would have been my age. As soon as he said Luzia, I knew that he was indeed the man I was meant to meet and I knew she was the reason why he was so angry. Our economy had taken a major hit with the energy crisis at that time but Portugal was in even worse shape and the couple felt they could do better here. He was a welder and pipe fitter and did get a job in Edmonton and later in Fort McMurray. They worked really hard, had two sons, bought a house, and were looking at building their dream home when Luzia got sick and was diagnosed with cancer. It was a rapid growing cancer and he quit his job to stay home and look after her. She passed away eight weeks after she was diagnosed and had been gone for a year and six months.

He told me that she was always a very spiritual person who believed in her angels and talked to them all the time. He said that he had never been a strong believer and after she died, he quit believing in God and angels. I understood then where the anger came from. He said he couldn't believe in a God that would take his wife after they had struggled so hard to get where they were. She always supported their church and was a help to any new arrivals who were struggling to build a new life in a new country. He was very angry because Luzia was such a good person and she was taken when some not nice people were still here. We ended up talking for two hours and I could feel him relaxing. We continued to meet at the dances each Saturday but I continued to refuse his invitations to supper. We had nothing in common except music and dancing and I was very uneasy around his anger.

Finally in mid-March I agreed to go out for supper with him and had a really nice evening. He relaxed a lot since we met and told me that he felt good with me and good about being able to talk about his life. We continued to see each other and I found myself enjoying his company very much which concerned me since we had nothing in common coming from two different worlds.

It was the end of April before I agreed to go to his home for supper and found out he was an excellent cook. As soon as I stepped inside the house, I could feel his wife's energy. It was furnished and decorated beautifully and he told me she was very artistic and had a flare for creating something from nothing. It was very powerful. I struggled not to cry and to stay aware of what I was feeling. All at once I understood it was she who brought us together and she needed my help to get him to let her go. He was a very perceptive man so he knew I was feeling something and I explained that I felt her presence. I knew that he had loved her very much and had not even begun to let he go. The house was like a shrine to her. I knew that if I was to help him, it would be a very difficult thing to do. When I drove home that night I knew and understood that I would have to love this man very much if I had any hope at all in helping him move on. In my mind I heard Reverend C. telling me that I had been called to serve and I heard Dr. H. telling me that I had a huge capacity to love which was a gift. It was about this time that another poem came to me as I was walking in the river valley.

BEGINNINGS

Guard your heart you said to me
I do not want to hurt you
I cannot promise anything
Empty promises are not true
Life and love hurts you said
But I've known those pains too
And closing off my heart
Is something I can't do
Life is meant to be a journey
Joy and sorrow hand in hand
Agony and ecstasy my friend
Are flowers in this land
While you think I may be hurt
I know I will have loved. You see
Whatever I am giving you

I'm also giving me
Just for today I'm asking you
Let your heart be free
Open up and clear your mind
And see what you can see.

It was a beautiful poem and really addressed the relationship I had with Tony. A few days later at the beginning of May, my granddaughter, Rhiannon, came to stay for the day. She was there to help me plant my bedding plants. She was four at the time and I loved having her with me. As we were digging in the dirt, words started to come so I ran,got a pen, paper, and recorded the following poem:

RHIANNON

She touched my hand
And my heart expanded
The colors of my world
Were suddenly brighter
She is a fairy
Rhiannon Faelyn
The name comes in a mist
Of purple, blue and white
Like a cloud
Of forever
Innocence

When I went back and read the poem, I started crying. It was so beautiful that it touched my soul like none of the others had. Rhiannon asked why I was crying and I told her because I was so lucky to have such a beautiful little angel in my life. I asked if she wanted me to read what I had written and she said, "yes, I love stories." She sat quietly listening to every word as I read the poem. When I was done, she told me that the story was about her and she really was a fairy which made me cry again. We made quite a picture sitting in the dirt, reading, crying, and laughing. I had the poem imprinted onto a beautiful picture and gave it to her when she was ten.

One morning in June, I woke up remembering a dream of a graveyard and the specific location of trees and roads. I had no idea what this was all about until Luzia came into my mind and I realized the graveyard was where she was buried in Portugal. I drew the graveyard as I saw it in my dream so I could show it to Tony. I had no idea how I was going to present this to him and knew it would upset him.

When I saw him the next weekend, I told him about the dream and also about Luzia's request for him to let her go. He became very angry which I expected; however, I never expected him to tell me that he never wanted to see me again. He left my place very angry and there was nothing I could do about it.

I didn't hear from him for three weeks. When I did I could tell from his voice that he had done a lot of thinking. He said he was sorry for getting angry at me and then told me that he would never believe as I did but he believed in me. From then on when we got together he would ask me if anything interesting happened. I never pushed him about getting on with his life because I knew he had to find his own way through his anger and grief. At the end of June, another poem arrived one day as I was reading one of my favorite books by Dr. Wayne Dyer.

THE LIGHT

What is it that I'm waiting for
Just beyond that opening door
I can feel it just beyond my reach
Something waiting sent to teach
Again the VOICE is calling me
And my soul is straining to be free
What is it that I feel
That is not here but seems so real
Where am I being led

Somewhere where my soul is fed?
I know that I am meant to see
What GOD and SPIRIT means to me
Once again the flame burns bright
And I sense a coming LIGHT
Awareness growing deep inside
With LOVE and PEACE
I shall not hide
And once again I say THANK YOU

One weekend early in August, I was walking to Starbucks to meet Bill and Darlene for coffee when the next poem made its arrival.

TRUTH

At the end of every day
All I really have is me
I had best respect and love
The image in the mirror I see
It is best to wear integrity
Up tight against my skin
It will keep me well protected
From life's lessons once they begin

Principles are another suit
I have always chosen to wear
They will last a lifetime
Treated with respect and care
There will be life's hard lessons
And we can all be led astray
But wear these suits
And wear them well
Truth of who really are
Will not be far away

I stopped to record the poem and after I read it received a message for myself. By the time I wrote this down and got to Starbucks, I was late. Bill asked me if I'd walked backwards. I laughed and explained what happened. At that point, I never discussed the poems with anyone so I explained that I'd been having messages come to me in the form of poetry and that they were very powerful. Bill asked if I would share the poem with them, so I gave them the page I had scribbled down. When he was finished reading it he asked if they were all as powerful. When I told him that they were, he said that there would be more but they were not mine to keep. They were meant to help not only me but anyone who read them.

By now Treva and I were getting excited about our upcoming trip to Turkey and I drove out to Camrose one day to talk about where we would stay and what we wanted to see. As I was driving another poem came to me so I pulled over to record the words.

AWAKENING

Can you see it
Do you feel it
Do you hear it
Can you touch it
Do you feel the colors
Rising from your soul
Does the music touch you
And the lightness make you whole
Can you hear the silence
And the hum from up above
That is awareness growing
And it only comes with love
Do you see the LIGHT
And feel it from within
That is the LOVE of GOD you feel
Now awakening can begin

By now I understood that these poems were road signs for me on my path to not only healing but to my purpose as well. Each poem offered wisdom and direction for me and were very, very emotional. I felt so much gratitude and humbleness, it was impossible not to cry. Seemed like I was always crying these days since everywhere I looked I saw and felt God. Another poem arrived in August as I stood in line at the bank waiting to get my Turkish Lira that I'd ordered.

THE LOOKING GLASS

You're not OK the way you are
You just don't look the "in" way
You'll never find the love you want
At least he'll never stay
You see your body's just not right
The hips too big and breasts too small

Your legs are just too heavy
In fact nothings right at all
You see the magazines and TV shows
Tell you what is the "perfect" size
The "perfect" shape the "perfect" body
And you're obsessed before you realize
That billions of dollars are being made
By people who don't care
That self hatred is a deadly disease
That can't be cured by the style of your hair
In the never ending quest of perfection
No one dares to look inside
Best to create the "perfect *façade*"
Than to face the things you hide.

This poem made a huge impact on me and showed me that I was on the right track in finally not caring what other people thought of me. I came to accept and love myself just as I was and knew that the "get beautiful" salons would never make any money from me. It made me even more aware of how shallow our society was becoming thanks to TV., the internet, and the movie stars that set the trends for how we should dress and look.

September sixth found Treva and I on our way to Turkey. We had a room booked for the first night in Istanbul and booked ten nights in Don's condo in Bodrum and the rest we would decide as we went. As we were preparing to land in Istanbul words were coming to me but I had no paper other than a napkin handy to write on. Treva wondered what the devil I was scribbling on napkins and then she realized that she was observing how the poems came to me. It was a long one so fortunately we had a few napkins handy.

I only had time to quickly read over what was written since we were starting the landing.

We were both tired and very excited since we didn't know what to expect. Getting through customs seemed to take forever, so I struck up a conversation with the couple ahead of us. I noticed their getting on the plane in Toronto so I asked if they lived in Turkey and were visiting Canada. They spoke English very well and told us that they were Turkish but had lived in Canada for many years and were back to visit family and friends. I asked where they lived in Canada and they said British Columbia. Then I asked where in B.C. and they said Vancouver, so then I asked what part of Vancouver. They asked if I knew North Vancouver and I said, "yes my son and family live in North Van" They then asked if I had ever gone to Deep Cove and I replied, "yes many times and loved it there." They asked if I'd ever been in the ice cream shop to which I replied, many times, I always take my grandson, Regan, there whenever I visit. They laughed and said that it was their business and we all hugged. It was an interesting moment and I thought that it was indeed a small world. It was a story my son and family found very interesting as well. When Treva and I finally got to our hotel and got settled, we had a chance to read the poem again.

THE ARRIVAL

Oh how my soul rejoices
I can feel the past coming home to me
This body has never known this place

But my soul is singing and feeling free
How exquisite the wondrous sensations
My eyes are beholding such beautiful sights
The music is caressing my soul with vibration
And my lips never tasted more fleeting delights
How can I put these feelings to words
I know few I can use to declare
The passion my soul is beginning to sense
Music not word is weaving a cloak I can wear
My eyes cannot see the mists that I feel
Gently swirling around my earthy being
But I have long since known and understood
My TRUTH comes from feeling not seeing.

Treva and I both found the poem very emotional. The use of words and imagery were new and I wondered if I was now channelling a different spirit. Again it spoke of my past lives. The trip ended up being a life changing experience for both of us. We were in Istanbul for four nights and during that time I felt what the poem had described. My feet were off the ground and I constantly felt an energy surrounding me. At times, especially when I was in the Blue Mosque, I felt like there were two of me; I was outside myself looking at another me. It was a very disoriented feeling and often I had the sense that I was "back home." One of the highlights of the four days was seeing the Sufi's dance which was amazing to watch. The other highlight was being invited by a shop owner to have the evening meal with his family.

When we left Istanbul we flew to Bodrum in the south part of Turkey. The condo that Don bought was in a small town outside of Bodrum and we took a bus to get there. The condo was in a beautiful gated community. It was a stand alone building of three stories with the basement level being a one bedroom suite. The main floor was a kitchen, living room, dining room, and two piece bathroom. The dining room had huge openings like windows but wooded shutters instead of glass. The top floor had three bedrooms and a large bathroom. From this level you could go to the roof which had a huge tank that stored water. From here you could see all the outlying area of fruit trees, olive trees, grazing areas with cows, and the beautiful Mediterranean.

We were here ten days and loved it. The water was warm, the sun was constant, and the people were fantastic. Most of the shop and restaurant owners could speak English since they learned it in school. The food was so good, always fresh from the sea, off the land, and off the trees. Everything tasted so much better than back home. We did so much in our time there and had so many interesting experiences that I can't tell you about all of them so I'll share just the highlights.

We took a five island sailing tour and met a young couple from Britain on holiday. We spent the day with them. At one point we got back on board and settled into chairs around a table as we started to sail to the next stop. We were talking about their families and jobs back in Britain when I felt a shift in myself like the other me had stepped forward. I started talking to the young fellow about things I had no way of knowing; personal things about him and his family. I remember his fiancée asking Treva what I was doing, how I knew these things, and I remember Treva telling her I was channelling. I don't remember anything after that until we were docking back where we started.

I talked to him for over an hour and Treva took the fiancée swimming while the boat was anchored in a cove.

Treva told me later that my voice changed, the way I held my body changed, and as soon as that happened, she knew I was channelling. I had to rely on Treva several times to fill me in on what happened when the other "me" took over.

One day she told me that the purpose for her coming on the trip was to be a witness to what I experienced. Treva took a few days to herself and ventured inland to an area called Anatolia where the Sufi's came from. I stayed at Don's spending time in Bodrum and in the little market places outside Bodrum. I was very drawn to the water in this area and especially to the water where Bodrum was located. I spent hours sitting on the beach and wading into the sea.

The history of Turkey fascinated me but the areas that I felt most "at home" were Bodrum, Ephesus, and parts of Istanbul. I think Treva had similar feelings in the interior areas since she was so excited when she returned.

After our time at the condo was up, we took a bus to a place called Selcuk where we stayed for several nights. We could walk from our hotel to Ephesus which is the site of an ancient Greek city built in the tenth century. It came under Roman rule shortly before the birth of Christ and was one of the seven churches of Asia that were cited in the Book of Revelations. It is here that the Gospel of John may have been written. I had done some research on the area before we came; but nothing could prepare me for the sight of Ephesus or for that matter Turkey.

It is a huge site under constant excavation so we spent four long days exploring everything . On one of these days we explored the amphitheater and it was here that I had another amazing experience. I climbed to the top of the seating area and Treva was standing on the stage. I could hear her perfectly. We changed positions and I was on the stage and she asked me to whistle a tune which I did. Just as I was going to walk off the stage I once again felt the sense of the other "me" coming forward. All of a sudden I started chanting the "Ave" mantra that came to me back in 2005 while I was having the *Kundalini* experience. I was aware of myself doing this but from outside myself. I watched as I chanted with arms outstretched and the other I could not interfere. I have a foggy memory of Treva clapping and telling me to "sing" it again.

After that I have no memory of what happened until I was bowing and then walking off the stage. Treva told me that after I chanted the second time, someone else yelled "again" so I did it again. After that Treva told me that all the workers shut off their power tools and the whole theater was quiet. I did the chant four separate times and then I bowed. I remember when I was bowing that I was looking at the theater full of people but it was from a different time. When I was walking off the stage, people were coming up to me and touching my arm and telling me that I was amazing and was thinking to myself but who was this "I?"

The rest of the day I felt very disoriented and like I was in a fog. Treva is similar in that she also feels energy so this was a very moving and emotional time.

We spent part of a day up high on the mountain at "Mother Mary's" which is supposedly the last home of the Virgin Mary. There is no mistaking the energy here and I don't believe that anyone could visit this site and not feel something. Treva has a friend who lives part-time in Turkey. She gave Treva the name of one of the Franciscan Monks who looks after Mother Mary's. We had the great pleasure and honor of meeting him and having tea with him in the monastery. We had a wonderful conversation with Father

Tarcey. He said that in his opinion, there would never be world peace until the religious leaders stepped away from religion and embraced spirituality.

We spent the remainder of our time back in Istanbul where we explored new sights. The day before we left we were walking around the Aga Sophia when another poem arrived.

ILLUMINATION

Aah Turkey, how do I say goodbye
The answers I have received thru you
Make me want to cry

I came expecting nothing, riches I've received
My experiences have humbled me
Enriching all that I've believed
I was told don't trust the people in that land
They are not like us and don't think like us
Until you've been there you will not understand
So I was careful but went with an open heart
And what I was told and what I found
Were miles and miles apart
So I asked a new found friend to me
How other people saw so much different
Than what I'd come to see
He smiled and said I'll tell you what I know
You have an open heart and love shines thru
It touches all and so begins to grow
What you have shown me
And to all I've seen you greet
Is only love and compassion
No judgment did I see
And so the one's you've reached out to
Have felt what you have given
And in tenfold given back to you
The moral of this little poem is a TRUTH you see
Love will be returned ten times over
Where and when it's given free

Both Treva and I were crying by the time we finished reading the poem because it summed up our visit to Turkey and left us both beyond grateful for the wonderful experiences we'd each been blessed with. We have been best friends since grade one; half a century of always being there for each other in the good times, and in the rough times. This time together gave us the opportunity to travel down memory lane and we had many moments of laughter which brought us many stares and smiles. It was a time I will cherish for the rest of my life.

2007

This was a powerful year for me filled with beginnings and endings, laughter and tears, agony and ecstasy. April brought a poem with a powerful message. By now the poems were no longer directed at me but at society as a whole.

SAVING GRACE

As mom is planning her weekend
While the kids are with their dad
The daughter is in the chat room
Ignoring the warnings she had
She has been meeting different people
It's a bit scary but exciting just the same
And besides she tells herself
She's only playing a game
Her friends have told her she's crazy
That there are weirdo's on the site
But she doesn't want to listen
Doesn't want to think they might be right
She's a very lost and lonely girl
Her parents' marriage has come apart
She and her sister are feeling

A dark and empty hole in their heart
She doesn't know which way to turn
She can see the pain her mom is in
Her father has lost interest in all but himself
And her sister is getting painfully thin
She feels enormous pressure to help
But she's still only a child herself
Fourteen is too young to carry such weight
By being an adult and putting child on the shelf
As she reads the message the guy has sent
Wanting to meet at a spot by the brook
One hand clicks off the computer
The other takes a card from her book
"Help line for teens" is what the card reads
She's so tired and scared and alone
She's drawn to meet the guy at the bridge
But she reaches out and picks up the phone
"Hello" says the soft voice from the phone
So warm and so filled with love
The young girl starts to cry and to talk
Somehow she knows help has come from above

"Saving Grace" was followed by "Innocence" in May and came to me when I was playing with my grandchildren in the park. The timing was perfect!

INNOCENCE

Children are a special gift
They are beauty to behold
They are joy and laughter to enjoy
And light the day as we grow old
I see the Creator every day
In smiles and eyes so clear
I feel the breathe of angels
As I hold the dear ones near
We must love and nurture these angels
And help them be all they can be
We have to help them find their wings
And be strong enough
To set them free
Tend to them like a garden

Love them and watch them grow
To be strong and true young men and women
In their actions their strengths will show
And before you know it
It will seem in the blink of an eye
The babies we held in yesteryears
Now nurture their own upon a cry

I was still seeing Tony and we had come to mean a great deal to each other. He was becoming less and less angry and he spoke with less judgment. One day at the end of June, he called excitedly while I was with client. When I called him back, he said that he'd seen a "for sale" sign in the window of a condo he wanted to view. He made an appointment to see it.

The unit was really nice and he really liked it; but it surprised me when he told the owner he'd pay a certain amount with no conditions. She looked at me and asked if he was serious and I said if he offered then he's serious. She asked for an hour to think it over and would call us with a decision. She called back in less than an hour and accepted his offer. I reminded him that he still had a property to sell. He just laughed and said, "I know a good Realtor who'll have it sold in less than a month." Since it was a Com Free I wrote up the offer for both of them free of charge and then listed Tony's place the next day.

He was right, it did sell in less than a month. He took possession of the new one a week before he had to be out of the old one. This gave him plenty of time to get moved and settled without rushing. The day I gave the selling Realtor the keys I knew my purpose was fulfilled. I could hear Luzia in my mind saying "thank you" and I could feel her slipping away.

This was the end of July and I knew I needed to tell Tony that our relationship was over but it took me until August before I could do it. He was upset and couldn't see why we couldn't stay together since we cared so much about each other. I told him it didn't matter that the love was there, the reason for us meeting was fulfilled and our time was up. I told him that there was a lady waiting for him and he would meet her before the end of the year. It was a very tearful goodbye and it hurt like hell.

I was happy with the progress that Tony had made but disappointed it wasn't as much as I'd hoped for. I felt like I hadn't done all I was supposed to but got a message that I had taken him as far as he was capable of going. I learned a very valuable lesson in that I could only guide and show the way. Even if I knew a person was capable of going further, it was they who had to do the work, I couldn't do it for them. Once again I was reminded of Dr. H. telling me about "the agony and the ecstasy." Since I always knew that I was only going to be in Tony's life for a short time, I never made a point of introducing him to most of my friends and family. Tara and family were the only ones who ever met him.

The weekend after I ended the relationship, Bill asked me to meet them for coffee on Whyte Avenue. I had told no one about ending the relationship because I wasn't ready to do so. After we finished coffee, we went separate ways but before we parted Bill hugged me which was totally out of character for him so I knew that he knew. I started to cry and told him I couldn't keep doing this. He just hugged and told me I'd do what I was here to do. At that moment I knew that I would be repeating this scenario; however, I also knew that at some point I would be released from this contract and would meet someone who would stay in my life. Shortly after that while I was walking in the river valley another poem came to me.

ENDINGS

Today has been a difficult day
A day that has been filled with pain
But illumination has had a cleansing effect
Like dust being settled by rain
Words are mere words
Intellectualized as we speak
But until we really feel these words
They are not our TRUTH to keep
So today I have allowed myself
To fully feel this pain
Because I fully understand
It will be replaced by knowledge I've gained

When we first met I felt a connection
Powerful from the start
But while I knew I'd be helping him
I am also learning from the pain in my heart
He is not responsible
For this pain I feel
My feelings are mine alone
And it is me that I must heal
I was sent this special man
His feelings weren't what I thought they'd be
But he was a beautiful soul
And meant no harm to me
Tomorrow is another day
The pain will be less in my heart
And when I am again all healed
Another lesson will start.

I was still running "Reaching Out" but government funding ended at the end of 2006. So for 2007 I had to book my own speakers which was a big problem since we had little money to work with. I turned to every professional person I knew for help. My lawyer, chiropractor, and accountant all volunteered to speak to the group, some more than once because of the interest. My chiropractor gave me the name of a medical doctor he knew that would be a good speaker. She taught mind, body, and spirit medicine as well as traditional western medicine and sounded like she would be an interesting person to meet.

I called her and we arranged to meet for coffee to discuss her "mind, body, spirit" workshop. I connected with her immediately and signed up for the six week workshop that was covered under Blue Cross. She only took eight students at a time and held the class once a week in an office downtown.

The first week was spent meeting the other students and talking about what we wanted to gain from the course. There was one man and seven women in the class and we sat in a circle. The first class Dr. G. gave us three sheets of paper and asked us to draw pictures representing what we thought we looked like in our darkest time, what we looked like now, and what we would look like when we achieved our goals..

The second week she started the class asking each of us how our weekend had been. The man in the class was sitting to my right and when it was his turn he said he's had a bad weekend. He'd had a restraining order placed on him by a woman in his building and he hoped that she die a terrible death. The energy I felt from him was unlike anything I'd ever felt before. A black cloud settled over me and I could feel myself shutting down to protect myself. It was a scary moment and then I could hear Dr. G. saying "breathe deep" and I knew she was talking to me. It was hard for me to focus on her, but when I did, I realized that she was looking straight at me and that I'd stopped breathing. It was hard to start breathing again because I felt like I was being smothered. However I slowly got my breath back and the darkness faded.

At the end of the class she said, "goodnight" to everyone but asked me to stay. When we were alone she asked what happened. She told me that I had risen off my chair at least six inches, then stopped breathing, and folded in on myself. I told her about the hatred and darkness I'd felt from the man and she told me I couldn't be in the class because of my ability to feel and see energy. She asked if I'd be okay with her coming to my house once a week and I agreed. I was thrilled with the chance to have her "one on one" for another four sessions and we had some very interesting conversations.

On one visit she suggested hypnosis and I agreed, forgetting my experience in Sedona. She had me focus on her voice and told me that I was walking on a secluded beach and would meet someone sitting on a log. When I met this person we would have a conversation and I would get answers to questions I had. I remember her voice at the beginning then nothing till she was shaking me telling me to come back.

Then I remembered my experience in Sedona and told her about it. She told me to never get hypnotized again, that it was very hard to bring me back. I remembered that once again I met Jesus but didn't remember anything else.

I had Dr. G. come to ""Reaching Out" a couple of times and everyone was grateful for the information and guidance she was able to give them. Since I felt such a connection to her I asked if she would take me as a patient and was grateful that she agreed. She has been my personal doctor ever since.

I often wondered how the man in her class was doing and if he would ever get out of the darkness. I knew he had dark energy but didn't believe he was evil. I have met other people with dark energy but have never met someone evil and pray that I never do. There are those of us who live our lives in the Light under the domain of God and there are those who live in the Dark under another's domain. Whenever I think on this subject I always remember my grandmother telling me to be careful what door I could open to the devil. It is far easier to fall under the dark domain than we think and even harder to get out from under it.

As far as I have been guided the only way out is for us to ask God for help . Since we have to be aware that we need help then want help before we can ask for it, we often stay in that dark place. We all want to be happy and we all want to be loved but what we all don't understand is that this love and happiness must come from self if it is to last. Once we learn to love ourselves we will love others and eventually we will find happiness within ourselves. This is a beautiful gift for ourselves as well as others.

Around this time I knew I needed some energy work done to clear some blocks but I only knew one person who did such work. Every time I went to call him, my friend Barb came to my mind. I finally called her and asked if she knew an energy worker and she did, so I got the name and number. I met Barb in 2005 and liked her right away. Her birthday is one day after mine and we had a lot in common. I came into her life to help her overcome some issues and we met several times a year to discuss where she was. She became a good client as well and I enjoyed my time with her both personally and professionally.

When Barb gave me the name "Sinead" all my senses were on high alert so I knew this was someone I was destined to meet. I called her and left a message with my name and number. When she got back to me and spoke, I could feel the same energy and she commented on it as well; telling me that my energy was so strong she could read me over the phone. It was wonderful talking to someone who I sensed was like me, so we spoke for over half-an-hour. She wasn't able to see me that week because an hour would not be enough; she wanted the afternoon free to see me.

My appointment was the following week and as soon as she opened the door, I was hit with this wonderful energy. I was looking at a beautiful woman with shocking red hair, cut in a really short, funky cut, bright eye shadow, and a smile from ear to ear. We hugged and it was like meeting the sister I never had. We both felt the connection and it was unlike anything I'd ever experienced before. She took me upstairs to her treatment room and as soon as I walked into it, my body was covered in goose bumps; the energy was so strong. She has a strong Irish accent and she said, "my god you've brought them all with you, this room is going to be crowded.".

I knew she meant that my guides were with me and I wondered if she had the ability to see them as well as feel them. I don't see people who have passed, I only sense them and communicate with them telepathically as I knew she did.

She is an intuitive healer which means that she has the ability to "see" and heal both the physical body as well as the spiritual one. The fascinating thing was that as she was moving around my body, I was channelling information for her. It was an amazing experience for both of us. At one point she asked what all the words were that she saw and I told her about the poems. She then said that they were not mine to keep, I was simply an instrument that God and angels could channel through. She told me that these poems would end shortly but others would come later. I was being told that the poems needed to be handwritten on sacred paper and kept in a sacred box. I ended up being there for over three hours and she refused to take payment beyond her one-hour rate because, as she said, she got a reading from me at the same time.

I would see her once a year and our sessions always went the same way. I also joined her healing circle which met on Sundays. Sinead showed me that I had the same ability as she did, but mine was not developed to the degree of hers. She was a powerful healer and I doubted that I would ever get there. But she disagreed and told me I had the power; I just used it in a different way. I learned a lot from her, she opened my mind, and helped me expand my beliefs. The day after I saw her another poem came to me while I was showing houses. There was no doubt it was meant for her.

A PRAYER FOR SINEAD

No matter where my wings may take me
No matter what the dream I see
No matter who my heart loves deeply
My soul belongs to THEE
AMEN

This was the only poem that ended with "Amen" and I knew that the poems which came to me over the past three years were about to end. I painted a page of water color paper with my water colors and then printed the poem on top and it turned out beautifully. I called Sinead and told her that I had something to drop off at her place and took it to her the next day. It was a very emotional moment when she read the poem. I was not sure what the words meant to her but she told me they had a very deep meaning and she taped the page on the door to her treatment room.

I now had the challenge of finding a sacred box! I had no idea what this box should look like or where I would find it. I just put in my order and waited. The following week I was guided to Michael's which is a craft store but not one that I frequent. I went with an open mind and wandered around the store without a clue what I was there for. I was going down an isle that was filled with scrap-booking materials and there it was . . . my sacred box. It was the only box on the shelf and it was covered in a black fabric and had a hinged lid that had a window in it. The inside was the same black fabric and it measured 8.5x10.5 inches which was perfect for 8x10 sheets of paper. I couldn't help but laugh at the situation. I then found some gold velum paper that I figured would be sacred enough and a calligraphy set to write the poems. There were twenty poems, so it took me a long time to hand print them all but they were finally done and stored in the sacred box.

I had always done the poems on Word, printed them, and put them in a binder that I had created. At that time I used the title of "Words of Light." Shannon happened to be back here on business around this time and he stayed with me. One morning I asked him how he slept and he said "not great. I read your poems last night and they kept me awake." No one had ever read them before with the exception of Bill and Darlene's reading of one of them. I kept them on the lower shelf of my coffee table so they weren't in plain sight. Shannon asked if anyone else had seen them and I told him "no," they had all been for me. He then told me that he believed they were not meant to be kept a secret and I should find a way of getting them out to the public.

On one of my visits to Sinead, I told her that she had a card with a man's name on it and she thought I should see him. She just laughed and said, "yes it's on my fridge but the time is not right yet for you to meet him."

Several days after that treatment, she called me with his name and number. I asked what he did and she told me I would find out. It was a few days before I felt the urge to call him. When I did he told me that he had no openings but then told me that he'd better see me that day. I had no idea what to expect when I got to his house. The door was opened by a man wearing dark glasses which I found strange but his energy was very peaceful and calming so I knew I was safe with him.

He introduced himself and led me down to the basement to a large room that he worked out of. It was filled with books, pictures, and pieces of sculpture all related to the beyond. I finally asked him what it was that he did and he told me he was a mystic the same as me. He then left the room to wash his hands and told me that I should open the *Book of Dreams* that sat on the coffee table and to remember the first word I saw on the page that the book opened to.

When he came back, he sat in a chair opposite me

and told me that the word I had seen was "Jesus" which it was. He then proceeded to describe my family to me in great detail which really surprised me. He described my parents, brothers, where I was raised, my ex-husband, and my children to a T. Once he did that he told me about myself, that I was here as a messenger as an instrument that God and the angels could work through. He saw the poems and told me there would be more and they needed to be published. He then gave me an outline of what the next five years would look like for me. When I look back on those years, they were filled with the events he foretold. He had written and published many books and I bought the one on dreams. It took him thirteen years to compile and was all channelled material. I have used it whenever I remembered my dreams and have found it extremely helpful.

In November of 2007 a friend and a woman that came from my hometown called to see if I would go down to Edgerton with her to a funeral. It was a lady from north of town that I didn't really know but I went anyway. During the service I noticed that one of the pallbearers had been a really close friend of my brother Bill when they were growing up. I remembered him well and also heard Bill and Darlene talk about him over the years, so I knew he lived in Comox, B.C. and knew that he was a Realtor.

During the luncheon I literally ran into him since I wasn't looking where I was going. When I saw who I'd run into, I said, "hello Jim." He looked at me, said, "I should know you but I can't remember you." So I re-introduced myself and then he remembered Bill's little sister. We talked for awhile, I told him I was in real estate as well and I brought him up to date on Bill and family. We talked about the market in Edmonton and then exchanged email addresses. I didn't want to keep him from speaking with others so I said "goodbye." The next time I saw Bill and Darlene I told them I had seen Jim and passed on a "hello" to them from him.

2008

One morning early in January, I woke up to a message for myself. I wrote down what was coming to me and then read it. It was not a comforting message. It told me that 2008 was going to be a transforming year for me both difficult and enlightening. It said I would be judged by someone close to me and would be called on to defend my beliefs and truth. This person would hurt me with accusations but I was not to judge in return, I was to return only love and know that I was protected. It told me I didn't have to justify myself to anyone, I knew who I was, and I lived my truth. I answered to God alone so long as I was doing His work.

I then remembered something that Rev. C. Said to me, "we both know who we work for." It was an uncomfortable way to start a new year and I knew I would need to be strong to deal with everything that was going to come my way. By the end of 2007 I decided that I would get the poems out to the public in some way and gradually came to see them as being in card form separate from each other and packaged in a wrapper tied with ribbon. I wanted the wrapper to be a picture and it needed to have a rainbow and a white bird in it.

In 2007 one of my long time clients moved to the interior of B.C. in the lakes area. She was a gifted artist and had given me one of her paintings as a "thank you" when they moved. I knew that she was the person to paint this cover and I emailed her and asked if she would. They were back in Sherwood Park for Christmas and I met to discuss the painting. I told her it had to have a rainbow and a white bird but that was the only criteria. We emailed back and forth regarding the "masterpiece" (as I called it) and by February she told me she was very frustrated because nothing was coming to her.

A week later she called to tell me it was finished so I asked what happened. She told me she'd been in her studio one morning and told herself she needed to think like me. She asked herself, "what would Lynn do" and then she asked her angels to show her what I needed. She put away the canvas and oils and got out water colors, sat down, and painted. She was really excited when she was talking to me and said, "now I understand what you experience all the time, it was strange because it was my hand holding the brush but it wasn't me who painted the picture." She told me that it was unlike anything she'd ever painted; wasn't sure that I would like it; and warned me not to expect anything that represented her usual style. She said she'd email me a copy then get a copy made and mail it to me.

I really didn't know what she could have painted that would be so much different that her usual work but I can say that I was really taken aback when I received it. Dorothy's work, whether in oils or water colors, is very real, almost like a photo and her detail is exceptional. What I saw was a watercolor that was in the style of Native American paintings and very simple. The background covering the whole page was a rainbow, in the forefront were wings outspread, and where the head would be are the tips of another set of wings and a head done in pure white. The larger wings had a lot of detail and the tail features were six rounded features painted blue. As I was holding and looking at it, I felt it had a lot of power. I put it on my fridge so I would see it, get used to it, and then I called my friend back. I told her I was very surprised at the work but I felt it had power and obviously had a story.

By March I knew the painting was telling me something but I didn't know what. Intuitively I knew that it could only be understood by a shaman but I had no idea where I was going to find one. By this time the person who was going to judge me had indeed done so with very hurtful words. When these judgements were being flung at me, I was very surprised at my reaction. I was absolutely calm, I didn't get angry and I didn't respond to the criticism. I sent love and light back to the person and cried when I got off the phone. I was deeply hurt but at the same time felt a protective shield come around me. I focused on how I was going to get the poems out and eventually decided that first I needed to understand the painting.

I made the decision to go to Vancouver to visit Shannon and his family then on to the Island to visit my other lifelong friend, Shari, my friend, Lynda who moved to Ucluelet a few years before, and Jim in Comox whom I met at the funeral in Edgerton in November. I knew that the answers I was seeking would be found on the Island but I didn't have a clue where or how I would find them.

I had a wedding in Red Deer at the end of April and spent

that night in Canmore. The next morning was beautiful. I
got up at five so I had an early start to Vancouver. As I was
getting ready to leave, I had a moment of anxiety since
this was the first trip to Vancouver without my grandson,
Kieran. Immediately I felt a presence over my right shoulder
and turned my head. In my mind I saw a beautiful eagle
so real I could have touched it. I remember the eyes of that
eagle looking into mine and I knew I would not be alone
this trip.

I spent a few days with Shannon, Lesa, and Regan and
then boarded the ferry to Vancouver Island to my next stop
at Shari's. I arranged to spend four or five days with each
of my friends and then head back to Shannon's. I found
Shari's place in North Saanich without any trouble and had
a wonderful few days reminiscing our youth, sightseeing,
and discovering quaint coffee shops and cafés. I had been to
the Island several times but never get tired of it as it seems a
world apart from the hustle and bustle of Edmonton.

Shari, Treva and I grew up together so the three of us
have been a constant in each other's lives for over fifty years.
Shari is a beautiful soul inside and out and we share the
same sense of humor so we laugh a lot when we're together.
She lived in the Middle East for over twenty years with her
husband, Allan, a pilot. She has seen and done things that
I can only dream about but she remains the same girl I grew
up with. If she were to meet you she would want to know
all about you since she has a very inquisitive mind and is
genuinely interested in people. She would have made a very
good detective.

When my time was up with Shari, I continued on to
Ucluelet; a place I had not visited before. I had been to
Tofino which wasn't far from Ucluelet on the west shore of

the Island. It was a long drive but very rewarding because the landscape was stunning, old growth forest with the biggest trees I'd ever seen, and always the smell of the ocean.

My friend, Lynda, bought her condo before she retired and rented it out. Once retired, she left Edmonton and took up residence in the small community on the ocean about twenty-five minutes from Tofino and separated by Long Beach. Tofino is the ultimate surfer's destination, Ucluelet is a fisherman's dream, Long Beach is a beachcomber's dream and the entire area is home to some of the most incredible storms you will ever witness.

Lynda and I go back many years since her son, Allan, and my son, Shannon, grew up together. She is a nature lover and it would be hard to find a more beautiful natural setting in all of Canada. The area has it all; old growth rain forest, sandy beaches that stretch for miles, hot springs, whales, fishing, surfing, great coffee shops and restaurants, and of course shopping. Tofino is much busier with tourists so if you like it quieter Ucluelet is the place to go. We spent hours hiking through the forest and as many hours beach combing for treasures. You can find lots of items both very old and newer that the tides wash in.

One of my most exciting finds was a massive tree that washed up on shore and remained where it was deposited. It showed the power of the ocean waves and tides and made me think I'd never want to get washed overboard. My time with Lynda ended all too soon and I was back on the road again to Comox. I had never been up this far north on the Island and everything was new to me. Again a long drive but as I got further north, I could feel a sense of excitement building. I knew that I would find my Native Elder up here somewhere, somehow.

I had shown the painting to both Shari and Lynda. Shari thought it was unusual and Lynda, the nature loving soul, was immediately attracted to it and she also believed I would find my answers in the Comox area. Comox is on the northeast side of the Island and is right beside Courtney. I called Jim when I was getting into Comox and he gave me directions to his place.

The next couple of days I spent exploring the area during the day while Jim was at work and he would show me more at night. On my second day there, I decided that the best place to ask about a shaman would be at a Tim Horton's since they were always busy. I went to a couple and the second one had several old timers having coffee together so I figured they'd be my best source of information. I got a coffee and sat not too far away from them, so I could observe them for a few minutes.

When I was comfortable with what I was going to ask, I approached and introduced myself. I asked them where I would find a shaman and when they asked why, I told them I had a painting that I needed interpreted. I brought the painting with me and when I showed it to them they all said at once "Campbell River." I had no idea how far away Campbell River was or how I got there but these old fellows were happy to show me and told me to go get my map which I did. They found a chair for me and I sat with them for about an hour getting directions and hearing lots of stories. It was a very entertaining afternoon and I shared the experience with Jim that evening.

I planned to head to Campbell River the next morning and I had a very strong intuition that Campbell River would hold many answers for me. The next morning at breakfast Jim asked how I'd slept and I said great except I saw feathers all night.

Jim gave me directions to follow from his place and I managed to get out of Comox and onto the highway without getting turned around. I was very excited and as usual I felt the eagle's presence over my right shoulder. It was only an hour's drive but very scenic so I took my time. About twenty minutes outside Comox I went past a large brown building complex to my left and as I drove by noticed a sign but never read it. As soon I passed I had a very strong feeling that I needed to stop there so I found a spot where I could turn around and head back to this complex. As I turned into the large parking lot I read the sign "Horsefeathers" and understood what my dream about feathers had meant. It was a large marketplace so I went into a shop that was filled with crystals, rocks, and gems and knew right away that I was in the right store. I wandered around the place and kept being drawn back to the saleslady who was busy with a customer.

When the customer left, I approached the lady and told her I was on my way to Campbell River and was compelled to stop. Being the kind of shop it was, I assumed she would be open to my approaching her and telling her I was a messenger with a message for her. She grabbed my hand and said, "I had a dream last night that my angels would send someone to me today." It was slow in the shop so I sat down with her and told her what I was meant to tell her. She wanted to pay me but I told her I never charged for the messages I pass on because it was part of my purpose and that I made my living selling real estate.

As it turned out she was the owner of the shop and gave me a large crystal and a turntable to place it on. I have it on top of my T.V. and as soon as my grandkids come in one of them turns it on. The round mirrored table turns and l.e.d. lights from below shine up through the crystal. It is very beautiful and the kids are very drawn to it. Anyway the stop had taken up over an hour of my time and I wanted to get to Campbell River since I had no idea where I was going. The road ran right beside the ocean and the view was beautiful.

As I came into Campbell River I noticed huge life-sized figures carved from wood. They were beautiful and I wanted to stop but felt I needed to find my shaman first. I drove through the city and as I was passing the museum, I had a very strong intuition it was here I needed to stop. I turned around and went back and into the museum. It was quite large, looked really interesting so I decided I'd go through it and paid my admission. As I did I knew the woman behind the counter was the person I needed to talk to. I went through the museum first and then stopped to talk to her. I asked if she knew of a shaman I would be able to meet. She asked why and I told her and then showed her the painting. She looked at me for awhile and then told me she could give me a name. She got a business card from her drawer, gave it to me, and told me that sometimes he never answers his cellphone.

I went outside, called the number, and a man answered. I told him my name and that I had come from Edmonton in search of a shaman who would be able to interpret a painting. He was quiet for a moment and then said he was just about to board the ferry to Quadra Island but it was obvious that the universe had sent me to him so he would meet me at the museum. I waited for a few minutes and a fellow walked off the road into the parking lot and I knew right away this was my man. Every hair on my arms was standing up, I had goose bumps, and there was an eagle circling overhead.

He walked right up to me and said, "Hi I'm Ollie," never asked if I was waiting for him, just said, "you are Lynn." We walked out onto the pier, sat down at a bench, and started to talk. He was chief of the natives on Quadra Island as well as a shaman. We told each other our stories and then I showed him the painting. He took it and looked at it for a moment and then said, "this is a masterpiece." I told him that I had always referred to the painting in that way. He told me that my friend was the only person who could have painted it because she believed in me and in her angels. He told me the same thing that she had, that it was her hand but not her that painted the picture. He then told me he was a visionary and that whatever answers I was meant to have would come through him at that time. He told me that the universe had been leading me to him since the year 2000 and then he told me what the painting meant.

It is something that I have not shared with anyone except my brother, Bill, and it is something that is not meant to be shared with anyone else. As usual I was crying and so was he so I asked him if I would ever be able to speak of God without crying and he said, "no, and neither will I." We had been talking for over two hours and his next ferry was due shortly, so I gave him a ride to the ferry terminal. We hugged goodbye with tears on our faces and then he said, "the eagle will take good care of you." I hadn't even told him about the eagle but he said it was one of my spiritual guides and would always be with me. His last words to me were "you will finish it" and those words are always with me.

I was running out of time but stopped to see the carvings and took a whole bunch of pictures. My favorite was a beautiful life-sized angel that looked so real it was eerie. By the time I got back to Jim's, he was home and getting the BBQ going. He told me that he was going to cook supper and I was getting fresh oysters which I had never tasted before. He wanted to know everything that happened that day, so after supper I told him all about my experiences. He is an old soul as well and is a believer in all I had to tell him. My time had come to an end and Jim helped me book my ferry for the following day. I would catch it in Nanaimo and get off in Horseshoe Bay. It had been an amazing journey and one that I would never forget.

When I got back to Shannon's, I told them about my time on the Island and about the sights I had seen along the way. As I was telling them my stories I realized how much I loved it out there and how fortunate they were to live surrounded with so much beauty. When I first told Shannon my idea for the poems he suggested I work with his graphics designed Monika, so I met with her the following day. I had taken copies of all twenty poems so she could get a feel for what they were all about. I explained that I wanted each poem on a card and I also wanted her to write her story on a card along with how she became involved with the project.

When I first arrived at Shannon's I kept calling Monika, Monique and Shannon had to correct me several times. We met at a restaurant in Deep Cove, North Vancouver and as soon as I met her, I called her Monique. Just as I was going to apologize I had a vision of her in a long, blue evening gown, her hair was black, and swept up, and held with fancy combs. She was young, very beautiful and was playing classical music on a beautiful piano for a room full of people who were also dressed up. I would think the time period would have been in the 1700's. When the vision ended, she asked if I was okay? I told her what the vision was about. Just as I finished telling her and before she could speak, I asked her what Machu Picchu meant to her because I had a message from someone tied to that place. She looked at me with a shocked look on her face and told me her favorite color was blue, she played the piano, loved classical music, the name Monique gave her goose bumps, her dad had recently passed away, and his favorite place on the planet was Machu Picchu. I was in tears as I gave her the message from her father but the whole experience was a great way for her to get to know the real me and it helped her with her designs for the poems.

I left the next day for my stay with Ron and Dorothy for a few day's in Blind Bay which is right on the Shuswap Lake in the interior of B.C. I was looking forward to seeing them and the home they purchased since they left Sherwood Park. It was another beautiful day as I set out and was so grateful for the great weather I had the entire time I was gone. I spent three nights with Ron and Dorothy and went boating, hiking, and laughing lots. Ron is one of the funniest men I have ever known and between him and Dorothy I was totally entertained.

I got to see the original "masterpiece" and told Dorothy she should keep it since she had such a powerful experience painting it. It was very rewarding for me to see how this journey of mine was touching so many other people's lives.

When I left Blind Bay I headed to Summerland and my last stop of the trip. I was staying with my friends, Ev and Reg. Ev had been with me at Royal Lepage for fifteen years and we always looked after each other's businesses when we took holidays. They retired the year before and bought a condo overlooking Lake Okanagan in the interior of B.C.

I really missed Ev at the office since she was impossible to replace. I spent a couple of nights there. We hiked and hit the wineries!!! Ev is a very spiritual person as well, so I was able to share my experiences with her.

My leaving was hard since this was the last day of my trip and I would be back home sometime late that night. Again I had perfect weather for the long drive home and stopped often to take pictures.

When I finally got home it was close to midnight and I had been gone for twenty-three days. That night I slept great but dreamed of doors and windows opening all night. That was telling me that more was going to be happening for me.

While Monika was working on the graphic design, I found a printer that I liked and priced everything out. I had no idea how many sets to print or how to get them out to the public. I decided that I would print 300 sets and find ways to sell them. I only wanted to recover the cost of paying Monika and the printer so I knew what I would have to charge for them. Monika sent me proofs of her design work and I was really impressed with what she created for each poem. Along with the twenty poems was my story, Monika's story, Dorothy's story, and a quotation I had from a Buddhist calendar. I found this quote years before and kept it because it touched me deeply and answered questions that I'd had for many years.

"In the spiritual world we must make a distinction between two kinds of loneliness. In the first we are out of touch with God and look for someone or something that can give us a sense of belonging and happiness. In the second the loneliness comes from an intimacy with God that is deeper and greater than our human senses can capture. We can think of this loneliness like blindness. The first comes from an absence of LIGHT, the second from too much LIGHT. The first we must try to outgrow with FAITH and HOPE. The second we must embrace in LOVE."

This made twenty-four 3.5x 8.5 inch cards that would be wrapped in an 8.5x 11.5 inch copy of the painting. I had three hundred sets printed and with the help of Caroline, Darlene, Treva, and Connie I got them wrapped and sealed in cellophane packages. Next I approached my doctor, chiropractor, naturopath, health food store, and two hospitals to see if they would allow me to place the sets of poetry in their places of business. I was elated when they all agreed. The ones I placed at the Cross Cancer and Gray Nuns were free. Over the next two years I also did poetry readings at several places and joined a book fair. The response was great and the comments that came back to me proved that Sinead, Bill, and Shannon were right in saying the poems needed to get out to the public. I realized this had been a test run for a book that I would one day have to write.

In June, while on duty at my office, a fellow came in wanting to see a Realtor, so I was called out front to meet him. As soon as we shook hands I knew that this was a highly intelligent man and an old soul. My intuition told me that I would have to be totally honest about myself including my spirituality and gift. We went into an office and he started telling me about the home he'd built on an acreage and to my amazement I was able to talk to him about construction. He commented on how knowledgeable I was. I hesitated, not sure what to say but again my intuition told me to be myself. So I explained that until we started having this discussion, I didn't know what I now knew. I told him that I was a very spiritual person and knew things that I had no way of knowing. I told him that information just came to me when I needed it. He laughed and rubbed his hands together and said, "my wife is going to love you."

I went out to the acreage a few days later to meet his wife and see the property so I could establish a range of value for it. His wife was much like me and we hit if off before we even spoke to each other. I went back in a couple of days, once I had established a value, and they listed the property with me. When I was leaving the subdivision I had a very powerful vision. I stopped the car, gathered my composure, and then called the wife. The vision meant nothing to me but I knew it would to her. I explained what happened and then gave her every detail of the vision. By the time I was done, she was crying. She told me the message was from her mom and what it all meant. When I give people a message or have a vision for them I am with them when they are very vulnerable. It is at these times that I am humbled and am reminded who I serve, always for the highest good.

Also in June Shari called to tell me that Curtis (her son) was getting married in December. The next day as I was ironing, Curtis' face came to me followed by a poem. This was the first poem I had since the others ended with "A Prayer for Sinead" back in August, 2007.

MY LOVE

I'm waiting for a special love
My heart once said to me
She'll arrive one day I know
And what I've longer for will then be
I do not care for wealth
I care not for what one can see
What I'm waiting for is deep inside
A seed, waiting to be freed
This seed will soon burst forth
A stunning bloom will then appear
But sweeter is the scent by far
Of knowing love that forever will be near

I called Shari to tell her about the poem and sent her a copy. She told me she was saving it until the wedding to give to Curtis. I found that the poem was different than the first twenty because it was meant for someone else. I also sensed that is was a different vibration and that made me realize that perhaps I was channelling more than one spirit. This made me even more aware of my intuitive side which I have always taken for granted since I have never been without it except for the six months or so in 2003 to2004.

I believe that we all possess this channel of intuition which is a spiritual channel (nothing to do with religion). It doesn't matter what race we are or where we come from or what our beliefs are. This channel becomes more open and clear as we evolve. As we evolve the purpose for our incarnations change and so does this channel. If our purpose here demands a higher intuitive level that channel is more open and clear. My channel is wide open although still not totally clear, some obstacles must still be overcome. I am a BELIEVER and have faith. It has taken many lifetimes to get to this place. I am an old Piscean soul and know that the only way forward for me is to overcome my fear of the unknown.

This fear is what holds us all back and it is only with discipline, truth, knowledge, and FAITH that we can overcome fear of the unknown. We all have fear to some degree but are not aware of it until we are in a situation that involves that fear. These fears surface when we are capable of dealing with them; however; we certainly don't feel that when we are fearful! Most of us don't recognize that we really don't have anything to be afraid of except the fear itself! It is a slow process to work beyond whatever we are meant to work through in any incarnation, but if we believe in ourselves, we'll get through regardless of how long it takes.

As Curtis and Andrea's wedding approached, Shari asked if I would read the poem at the reception. I know that I cannot read or talk about any topic where I feel God without crying, so I told her I wouldn't be able to read it without making a mess of it. Shari later suggested that I read it at the end of the program and if I got into trouble the M.C. would finish it, so I accepted.

The wedding was December twentieth, 2008 in a white Victoria with snow covering the ground. The ceremony was lovely and soon it was time to read the poem. I found I wasn't overly nervous and managed to get through to the last few words without crying. I made the mistake of looking at Curtis at the end and he was crying. Needless to say the last few words were mixed with tears. Shari would later tell me that when I started to read the poem the room became totally silent. It really touched my soul when I had people come to me later to tell me they loved the poem and to ask if I wrote poetry.

As the day progressed so too did the storm which was forecast. By midnight it was a real blizzard and I had concerns about the ferry running in the morning. In the morning I decided to catch the first ferry and had Dave (Shari's sister Caroline's husband) drive me to the terminal. As it turned out it was the only ferry that ran that day as the storm got worse and the ocean got really rough. That was the worst ferry trip I have ever made and spent part of the trip in the bathroom getting sick.

Shannon picked me up and we managed to get back to his place without getting stuck in the snow but vehicles were stuck everywhere. Vancouver is not equipped to deal with a storm of this magnitude and much damage took place. A good part of the North Shore was without power and shopping centers were closed. The only store that managed to stay open was Walmart because they have their own generators for power. Four days to Christmas and the storm was a disaster with terrible wind along with the snow. Huge trees were torn out by the roots and some fell on roads and homes. Shannon's area never lost power but people were stuck everywhere.

By the twenty-second the storm had passed, the snow ended and started to melt. We were unable to look at Christmas light displays because of the snow. It wasn't cold so we walked to a few places to see the lights. It was really very beautiful with all the snow but the storm had done a huge amount of damage. Christmas Day was white and the roads cleared enough so Lesa's family could make it for dinner.

Boxing Day I woke up with the urgent feeling I needed to walk to the coffee shop in the little shopping area about twenty minutes from Shannon's. I wasn't even sure the coffee shop would be open but I got dressed and headed out at eight, while everyone else was still in bed. It was a long, hard walk since the sidewalks still had a good foot of snow on them. At least the snow was light and not the heavy wet stuff that was in Victoria. I finally got to the coffee shop and not only was it open, it was also nearly full. I got a coffee and muffin and managed to get a table where I sat wondering why I was led here.

About ten minutes later a young woman, maybe late twenties asked if she could sit at my table since all the other tables were full. As soon as she spoke, I knew this was who I was to meet. I asked her to sit and asked her name. She was British and said she and her father were here for Christmas to be with her brother and family who happened to live about four blocks from Shannon's. She told me that her mom passed away in the spring and her dad wanted them to be with her brother for Christmas. As soon as she told me her mom died, I knew why I was there and asked what brought her out this early. She said she'd had a really strong feeling she needed to come to the coffee shop but didn't know why. I took her hands in mine and explained that I was a messenger. She started to cry and said, "my mom guided me here didn't she?" I told her "yes" and then passed on the messages. It was very emotional and she cried while I struggled not to. When her mom told her she loved her and said goodbye I cried with her.

When I got myself under control, we continued our conversation. She told me that she was studying law and wanted to become a lawyer. Once she was done she and her dad would move to Vancouver to live. The law firm that I used and also have referred clients to had a British conveyancer who was fantastic at what she did. She told me that in Britain, she'd obtained her law degree but couldn't practice in Canada as a lawyer, so she was a conveyancer. I explained this to the young woman, got her name and email address, and promised I would have Mandy contact her to advise her on the process she would need to practice in Canada. We said "goodbye" and I trudged my way back to Shannon's where I found everyone up and making breakfast. I briefly told them why I was out so early and that the sidewalks were knee deep in snow in some places. It was an interesting Christmas and a great way to end 2008.

2009

In January I met with Mandy, the conveyancer, and told her about my experience in Vancouver at Christmas. She said she would be happy to help so I gave her the young woman's name and email address. Mandy called me several days later to tell me she contacted the woman and gave her all kinds of advice in regards to practicing law in Canada. I never keep names or contact information unless I am specifically guided to do so. In most cases these are one time meetings and I will never see the people again. I had one fellow ask me what would happen if the person I was to meet didn't understand or believe and I told him that no one would ever be placed on my path unless he or she was in search of answers and able to understand my messages. I was simply the messenger, the instrument used to deliver the message they were to receive.

By the end of May, I was exhausted and struggling to come to terms with everything that had happened since 2003. I needed time to myself and decided to take a few months off work. I knew financially this would hurt but knew there was no choice. I made a plan and had a long talk with my angels and guides. Looking back on that time now, it was truly amazing how my calls stopped and I was free to begin the healing work I needed. I told my office what I was doing but no one else.

Nature is God's pharmacy, so I immersed myself in nature. I walked for hours in the river valley exploring trails I had never been on before. I was drawn to the Edmonton River Valley since the first summer I worked for my aunt on 124 Street back in 1964. The valley trails were free from electromagnetic smog and the air pure and fresh. I lost myself for hours walking and stopping now and then if I was close to a coffee shop. I have always known that I was protected and would be taken care of, so I wandered carefree and open to all the healing messages that were coming to me. I spent time with people who needed my help and people showed up to help me.

In August, my grandson, Kieran, and I once again drove to Vancouver. Kieran was going camping with Shannon, Lesa, and Regan; and I was going to house and pet sit for two weeks. I was thrilled since North Vancouver is a very special place for me. I have felt a powerful connection to the area since the first time I went there when Shannon and Lesa moved into their new home in July, 2001. I was so excited I was like a kid in a candy shop. So many places to explore, so many pictures to take, and so many people to meet.

One morning I woke up knowing that I needed to go to the Bay in Park Royal, the largest shopping center on the North Shore. It was not what I had planned for the day but the shopping center is situated at the beginning of the sea wall that runs a little over four kilometers along the ocean to a quaint village called Dundrave. Since I never really know where I'm going to meet the person I'm suppose to, I wandered around the store paying attention to my intuitions. As I approached a perfume counter, an older lady was finishing her purchase of some perfume she had sampled. I found the aroma intoxicating, so I stopped to find out which brand it was. There were two women behind the counter; one was small and dark, the other was tall and blonde and looked sick.

Before I even had a chance to speak, the dark one asked me if I was a "seer." I was familiar with the word and knew she was Persian since seer is a term used in the Middle East instead of psychic. I told her that I was a messenger. I also said that I was interested in the perfume the lady ahead of me had bought. She told me the name and gave me a card with some sprayed on it. I really liked it so I bought some. I knew that the dark woman was not who I was meant to meet but I wasn't sure about the blonde. I knew something was bothering her but had no messages or intuitions for her.

Just as I was turning to leave, the blonde touched my arm and asked if I had a message for her. I told her I didn't. She looked very disappointed but I had nothing to tell her so I left the counter and the Bay. I had walked maybe ten feet when words came to me with a force that took my breath away. I knew immediately they were for the blonde, so I went back to the counter and told her I'd just received some words, not much of a message. Then I told her the words, "everything will be alright" and she started to cry. She told me that she'd been telling herself that for months but everything was not alright. I had no other words for her and even though I knew she was in pain, there was nothing I could do.

As I turned to walk away again, I reached my hand out,

and touched her arm. The strange thing was that there was a force that lifted my arm and placed my hand on her arm, I didn't do this, it was as if my arm had a mind of its own. I felt a strange vibration running up and down my arm. This was a first for me and the next thing I knew I was saying to her, "He wants you to know everything will be alright" This time we were both crying and so was the dark lady. I'm sure if anyone was watching, they'd wonder what the hell was going on over there! I finally said good bye to both them and left.

My arm was still tingling and my fingers were numb. I headed out of the shopping center down to where the sea wall walk started. The fresh air felt great and I was anxious to clear my head. About half-an-hour later words started to come to me so I took out my paper and pen and started writing. When the words stopped I read what I had written. It was another poem and it was for the blonde lady. I continued walking until I got to the end of the wall. Then I found a coffee shop, got a coffee, and sat down to rewrite the poem for her. She was in a lot of pain and the words I had written came with a very high vibration and a lot of love. It was very emotional just re-writing it.

EVERYTHING WILL BE ALRIGHT

My heart keeps whispering
These simple words to me
I know not from where they come
But I trust they'll help me see
Everything will be alright
Are the words the angels sing
They do the Lords bidding
And LOVE and LIGHT they bring
Everything will be alright
Is what HE says to you
The words are full of GRACE
And meant to see you thru
Whatever turmoil your heart and soul
Are deeply troubled by
One day will pass and LIGHT will shine

And LOVE will light the sky
Everything will be alright

I finished my coffee and headed back to the Bay at Park Royal. When I got there the counter ladies had been replaced with new ones so I left the poem with one of them. I never leave my phone number but this time I felt I needed to. I quickly wrote my cell phone number after my name then folded the paper up and gave it to one of the women. I told her it was very important and was to be given to the blonde woman who was working the previous shift. I had no way of knowing if the poem would get to the blonde or if the lady would read it. I trusted that it would get to where it needed to go.

In June 2014, my cell phone rang one night and when I answered, a woman said, "I don't know if you'll remember me but I was working in the Bay in Park Royal, North Vancouver in August, 2009. You had a message for me in the form of a poem. I just want to thank you for that poem and tell you it got me through a very difficult time and I have it close to me all the time." I was so surprised, when I finally recovered we had a wonderful conversation. I told her I was headed back to North Vancouver in August and arranged to meet her when I got back. We did meet and I got the whole story five years after I first saw her.

During the same trip to Vancouver in 2009, I spent a day at Granville Island. I spent a few hours walking along the waterfront looking at the condo complexes which are so unique and different from what is built back in Alberta. I love this area and it would be wonderful to live in any of the complexes that face the water. It's easy to spend a few hours here especially when the weather is great. I wondered back to the marketplace for some lunch, and found a table in the small, upper level that allows a view of the water.

The smells and noises are unique to the area with the waterfront, restaurants, market place, sea gulls, people, boats, and traffic. Only one place like it in Vancouver and the tourists love it! I had taken a free Granville newspaper and read as I ate. One page had ads for the different businesses and one of the ads read: VANCOUVER'S BEST PSYCHICS ARE ON GRANVILLE ISLAND. I took note and thought to myself, that's interesting.

When I was clearing my table, the newspaper slipped and fell on the floor, landing open to the page with the ads. My eye was drawn to the ad about the psychics. This got my attention so I tore the page from the paper, folded it, and put it in my backpack. I wondered around the market for awhile and then left to explore the waterfront again. As I left the market, I found myself turning in the direction opposite of where I had planned to go. I crossed the street and was walking along the walkway when I suddenly tripped and fell against a glass door. I looked at the walkway and there was nothing that I could have tripped on. As I started to walk again I glanced at the door and there in big black stenciled letters was "VANCOUVER'S BEST PSYCHICS UPSTAIRS." I climbed the stairs telling myself if someone could see me right away I would see them. The top landing opened into a large, well-appointed reception area complete with familiar music, familiar scent of a blend of essential oils, and a small water fall feature. It was very pleasant and I took everything in as I approached the receptionist.

I asked if someone was available immediately for a reading and she said "yes" as she picked up the phone to announce me. There was a hallway to one side with doors opening into it and one of the doors opened and a tall, beautiful woman with long black hair stepped into the hall and came towards me. She shook my hand and introduced herself and then told me that she would normally be gone but her guides told her to stay to meet someone.

It was a very interesting thirty minutes and again, as when I met Sinead, I had messages for her as well. She asked why I didn't work as a psychic because I would be very successful. I told her that real estate worked for me because I could go where ever I was guided and wasn't hindered by a nine to five job. She had some interesting information regarding the poetry and the upcoming year. Then she told me that being me wasn't always easy since I was here in a physical body but had one foot on the spiritual plane. Since the year 2000, I had been "fast tracked" which meant two life times of experiences and information were being sent to me in the last half of this lifetime. This was why I sometimes got exhausted and overwhelmed and wanted to go *home*. She told me her guides were stressing the importance of my spending time outside as close to trees, water, and mountains as possible. This explained my attraction to the river valley in Edmonton and my need to spend time in North Vancouver. She refused to take payment for the reading, just as the psychic in Sedona had done.

Shari called me in October to tell me her first grandchild had arrived. I could tell she was really excited about this and was planning a trip east as soon as possible. A few days later the poem "Miracles" came to me.

MIRACLES

Tiny hands and tiny feet
Arrive fresh from Heavens door
Another of Gods masterpieces
Of that we can be sure
One is never quite prepared
For what this tiny bundle brings
These emotions are unknown
As our hearts and souls sing
When first that tiny hand
Grabs our finger and our heart
We are wonderfully amazed
That what we feel is not that far apart
From what we've been told and what we've read
About the LOVE from up above
And we are at last blessed
With the TRUTH of LIGHT and LOVE

I called Shari to tell her about the poem and emailed it and she set a copy to Curtis. This poem was published in 2010 with The Poetry Institute of Canada.

2010

January fifteenth I once again was blessed with the gold light just as I was waking up only this time it lasted only a few seconds and then I opened my eyes. I have often thought back to this moment as to whether I was actually awake. I know that I saw my room from my pillow and didn't move to get up. The room was light enough to see my dresser and pictures on the wall. All at once, I saw a black shape rising from the foot of my bed. It scared the hell out of me and I found I couldn't move. I could only watch this shape rising until it reached the ceiling and covered the wall. It was the image of a Phoenix, I was so scared I could hardly breathe. Then I heard the word, "Faith" and the image was gone.

The room was so cold I could see my breath and I was trying to make sense of what just happened when words started to come. I got up, got the book and pen from my nightstand and started writing. It was only four lines. My room had warmed up by this time and my breathing was back to normal. I got dressed, had something to eat, and headed out the door.

Over the next four hours the entire poem appeared and when put together, I was stunned. I knew at once it was for my son and myself because we share the same birthday. I also understood that there was a strong message for me here in that I sometimes must put aside my questions and replace them with FAITH. This is something my brother has been trying to teach me. I'm a slow learner but the image of that Phoenix made an impact. Faith is believing when it is beyond the power of reason to believe and while I do have faith I do not have FAITH . . .yet!!!

PHOENIX RISING

Within the soul of man
There dwells the source of LIGHT
But in that same place
Absence brings the dark of night
Two wolves battle deep within
Both hungry to succeed
In the end the one to win

Will always be the one you feed
The fish are as old as time
Indeed the wise souls of the land
The metal tiger is strength and courage
And is there at your command
Fish and metal tiger
Are indeed a part of thee
But the Angel stepping forth
Is who you now must come to see
We have wrapped our wings around you
And always kept you from harms way
Time now for you to spread your wings
Where you have been you could not stay
You are there to spread the LIGHT
The dark can be no part of you
Wisdom, strength and courage
Are there to see you thru
You will be shown the path to take
A door will open and you will see
Do not fear or underestimate your path
Trust in what you are there to be
It is your soul's destiny
To be what you must be
And should you feel the darkness
Know we are always guarding thee

As I read the poem, I felt its power and for several days I
reread it to understand what it was telling me. The elements
of past lives were very obvious. The two wolves came from
my past life as a Native Shaman; the metal tiger from my
life as a Buddhist; Pisces is my astrological sign represented
by two fish. My birthdate is represented by the metal tiger

in the Chinese zodiac. The Latin word for messenger is angelus. The reference to "two wolves" is reference to the true self and the shadow self (or to God and to Satan) and the fact that whichever one we feed creates the domain under which we live. This was powerful and had a sense of urgency that made me aware of how neglectful I had been in regards to my purpose. This was partly due to fear and partly due to procrastination. I could understand why at times my brother was so frustrated with me and I vowed to focus more on my purpose. I emailed the poem to Shannon as I believed it was also meant for him.

February first I woke to words and quickly grabbed pen and paper. I was very unsure as to whether I should include this poem since it was very intimate. Each time I decided not to include it, I had a powerful sensation in my crown chakra and a strong sense that this was the wrong decision so in the end I included it.

SOUL MATES

The agony of ecstasy
Coming to me from some distant shore
Please Lord I pray, lighten these emotions
Please Lord I pray, bring him to my door
The agony of ecstasy
Is something I know well
Please Lord I pray, I've waited so long
Since lifetimes past my soul could tell
His touch as his arms went around me
His touch as he gently kissed each cheek
So much feeling beyond any word
The flood of this passion is making me weak

Few men I've ever met
Have been of interest to me
Most of them when interested
Cannot look beyond what they choose to see
It has taken a very special man
To see the truth of me
To give me back what I can give
To undo the chains and set me free

The notation I made at the time these words came to me was, "I recorded this February first, 2010 but don't know who it's for. Perhaps it's for my future self . . .it feels like it's mine." I was turning sixty in February, and decided not to be here but had a hard decision on where to go. In the end I asked my travel agent where he had been recently that he liked and he told me that he and his wife had been to an all-inclusive in Puerto Vallarta, Mexico. Since I'd never been there I decided to go for only one week and I booked it.

On the morning of February twentieth, I woke up remembering a very vivid dream. I seldom remember dreams and when I do they are always prophetic. My daughter, Tara, was taking me to the airport. When she picked me up, I told her about my dream and that I would be meeting a man in the airport's luggage carousel, but didn't know if he was coming or going.

It was a late flight and I got into Puerto Vallarta close to midnight and was tired. I was waiting for my luggage and asked the woman beside me where I went next since I didn't remember the airport from the time I'd landed there in 2007. She asked where I was staying, so I told her and heard a man's voice from my other side say, "I'm staying there too." I turned to see who was speaking and knew immediately that this was the man from my dream. The first thing I noticed was the energy, then the eyes that were so much like my dad's. Because we had booked with different travel agencies, we had different taxis but met up again at the check in and agreed to meet for breakfast.

The next morning I found out his name was Don, he was retired, and lived in Edmonton. A week didn't give me much time to explore Puerto Vallarta but enough to know I wanted to go back. It was enough time to get to know Don a bit. I found out he was originally from P.E.I. which was where my maternal grandparents came from. Even with the distance between Alberta and P.E.I. we found out that our early lives were very similar. We both grew up on farms and knew what it was like to work hard. We had a lot in common and spent time together when I wasn't exploring the area. We exchanged phone numbers and agreed to get in touch once he got back to Edmonton. We've enjoyed a great relationship ever since our first meeting and he fits well into my family.

In July my co-worker and friend, Don, got married. Back in April he and Laura announced their marriage and a few days after the announcement, these words appeared.

THE UNION

Thru the mists of time
Thru the veils of Light
These souls were brought together
Sights, sounds and love unite
Their hearts they found among the stars
Their vows were written on the sun
Their love has withstood many trials
And now they stand as one
Words can never really be spoken
When one look can say so much
All that is meant to be conveyed
Can be felt in just one touch
What the universe has brought together

No man can put aside
For what love can bring to light
Is where these souls reside

When I read the poem I was really touched, probably
because I knew Don and Laura, and definitely because of
the bond I felt with Don. I never gave them the poem
until the day before the wedding in July. I printed it on
gold velum paper, rolled it up, and tied it with a satin
ribbon. I gave it to Don at the office and told him to read
it with Laura.

The day of the wedding, after the vows, I was going
through the receiving line and Don told me that the poem
was going to be read at the reception. He asked if I was
okay with the M.C. telling everyone who wrote it, and I
said "yes." When the M.C. said he had a special poem to
read, he said that the poem touched him when he read
it. I had a number of people I know come up to me later
and comment on the beautiful poem, so I knew that these
poems would touch many people and there was a purpose
to their being published together.

August 2010 found me flying to P.E.I. to meet Dons family
and to see where my grandparents had come from. Just as
we were getting ready to land the first four lines of a poem
came to me. This was Dons introduction to how the poems
came to be. The rest showed up a few lines at a time over
the next 2 weeks. The holiday was great but just a taste of
what the Island had to offer. I spent a few days looking up
my grandmother's history in the archive building and I spent
time with Dons sisters and their families. I knew before I
even left that I wanted to go back. By the time we left I had
the whole poem and it was beautiful and very touching.

COMING HOME

Shadows dance on sun struck clouds
Fresh sunrise colors shout out loud
We bring you beauty to start your day
We bring you Light to show the way
I gaze upon sand dunes sliding gently to the sea
And know there is no place on earth I'd rather be
Than in this sanctuary that makes me smile
At red sand beaches stretching mile upon mile
Red cliffs rise out of the blue
The color of the waters and the bright skies too
Moisture laden heat wraps me tight
And will hold me long into the night
Do you feel the peace this place brings to me
Can you see beyond the beauty of the land and sea
Is your soul renewed and your spirit light

Do you feel everything in your world is right
The healing and nurturing have been received
        once more
From this timeless land of red cliffs and shore
You can now return from where you came
Knowing coming home has worked its magic once again.

When I read this poem, I am immediately connected to my grandmother. I can see her in my mind and can smell her lavender powder that she always wore. I know she would have loved this poem as well. When I got home and printed the poem on Word, I gave Don a copy and emailed his niece a copy. She is the same age as I and we really got along well. She told Don that the poem could only have been written by a native Islander. It was published in 2011.

2011

I went back to Puerto Vallarta with Don in February and spent three weeks this time. While my life was going very well, a good friend of mine was struggling with hers. Her marriage ended in 2010 and she was having a hard time adjusting. In April words appeared and once I read them, knew they were for her. I printed the poem on Word and sent her a copy. It was a very strong poem with an equally strong message and it brought back memories of when I was in such a dark and scary place. It made me very appreciative of my growth at this time in my life. It also brought me very close to Caroline because I knew what she was going through and I could feel her pain.

KEEP THE FAITH

Sometimes our path is filled with LIGHT
Sometimes the Light is hidden by pain
We must always remember the LIGHT is not gone

And will return with the knowledge we gain
If we can keep that Light however dim
Alive although veiled with the uncertain
There will always come a day in a brighter tomorrow
A much larger window and an open curtain
Belief is the key and the only way
That the LIGHT can illuminate all
This gift is bestowed on all of mankind
And matters not how big or how small
What do you choose to do with your life
Do you live in the dark or in the LIGHT
You create the world in which you live
It matters not if you're blind or have sight
What you project is what you'll get back
Anger brings anger and hate will bring fear
That is the secret and will never change
What's in your soul and mind is what you'll have here
We must see our world from deep within
It is our soul that sets us free
Have the mind and the soul both seeing the same
And your world can become what you want it to be

In July I met a client at an acreage I had sold her and her future husband. He is my accountant and has been for twenty plus years. I met his future bride back in the spring when they decided to buy some acreage together. She was a nurse and a really easy person to like and have fun with. I had a great time showing them properties and was really happy that they were able to find the right place.

Gerald was unable to be with Beth when "possession day" came, so it was just Beth and myself walking through. She was very quiet, not her usual self and then I realized I hadn't seen her big chocolate lab. When I asked where she was, Beth began to cry and said she had to put her down. The dog was getting old and Beth had her since she was a pup, so they were together for a lot of years. When I first met Beth, I met the dog as well. She was a lovely dog, very smart and it was easy to see the bond between the dog and Beth. I felt bad for Beth because I knew what it was like to lose a dog that was a long-time, faithful companion.

As I was driving out of the subdivision, words came to me so I stopped and recorded them. When I went back and read them I cried and I knew they were for Beth.

A GIRL'S BEST FRIEND

You cannot see me
But I'm still here
While you are grieving
I'll stay very near
You can grieve for me
For a little while
Then let me go
Remember me with your smile
I'll be with you

In the morning sun
And I'll be with you
When your day is done
Let me rest
With the flowers bright
I'll still be here
With each new light

When I got home I input the poem on Word and printed it on the gold velum paper I keep for my poetry. I mailed it to Beth along with a letter telling her how it came to be. I got a call a few weeks later thanking me and telling me it helped her deal with the loss. The poem was published in 2012 and it is a poem I have given to several people when they have lost a loved one, be it a pet or a person. I have always been told that the poem helped. 2011 ended with Don and I making plans to return to Puerto Vallarta once again in 2012.

2012

In early February, I woke up one morning with words running through my mind, so I grabbed pen and paper and started writing. As always, I have no idea what it's really about until I can go back and read it, nor do I know who it's for. Once I read this one I knew it was for a long-time friend who was struggling to find answers to the problems she was encountering.

Leona and I have been friends for forty plus years and have been through our ups and downs together. We can go months without seeing each other but when we do, it's like no time had passed. We trust and respect each other and have always been honest with each other. She is one month younger than me and is forever young at heart. Her hair is wild,... short, reddish blonde with a purple streak in the front (her signature color) and she has an amazing mind for business and making money. I called and told her I was emailing her something important and when she called me back she was crying. She asked how the right words show up for the right people at just the right time and I told her, "I don't have the answers, I just record the words."

143

The truth is that her angels work through me the same as other peoples' do. I have accepted that I am here to serve whoever, however, and whenever I can, in the name of God, always for the highest good of all.

SEARCHING FOR ANSWERS

Love and Peace are with you
And the angels hear your prayer
Although you feel you are all alone
You are always in Gods care
Sometimes it seems it's always dark
Nowhere can you find the LIGHT
There are no answers you can see
No putting wrongs to right
It is in that time of darkness
That we are closest to the LIGHT
It is the clouds of anger, fear and loss
That keeps it from our sight
There are always lessons
That we are here to learn
It's not understanding what they are
That causes much concern
Time will bring a new awareness
Of what you've just been through
And the Love and LIGHT of God
Will bring you life renew

Don and I spent three wonderful weeks in the sun and
sand in February and March then I was off to Vancouver
to spend spring break with Shannon, Lesa and Regan.
Whenever I am there Regan and I spend hours hiking and
exploring the trails through North Vancouver.

On one of our explorations I suddenly had words
coming to me and no paper or pen. I didn't know what to
do and then intuitively told my angels that they needed to
remember these words for me so I could write them down

when we got back to the house. I said them out loud as they came to me and prayed this would work.

It was a couple of hours before we got back to the house and as we walked into the kitchen, I said to Shannon and Lesa, "Don't talk to me and give me a pen and paper." They looked at me strangely but did as I asked and as soon as I put the paper on the counter, the words came back. I had to write like a demon since the whole poem was coming at once. When it was finished Lesa asked what just happened, so I told her. I read the poem and then gave it to them to read and once again, Shannon told me I needed to do something with the poems. I found this poem to have a different vibration than the others, it just felt different and once again I wondered if I was channelling yet another spirit.

SPRING COMING SOON

Rain soaked tree stumps
Wearing coats of green
More moss grows here
Than I've ever seen
Guarded by ferns
And blackberry thorns
Like angry young bulls
With razor sharp horns
Light filters thru
Branches naked and cold
I wonder thought I

What secrets they hold
Do they remember
Warm summer days
When their leaves
Would dance in mysterious ways
Did they call to the birds
Come build your nest here
I'll keep you safe
And your friends will be near
Do they remember
Warm summer nights
When blossoms would show
The most colorful sights
The blackberry bushes
Heavy with bloom
Showing the promise
Of sweet fruit coming soon
All of these memories
From days and from nights
Now see the coldness of winter
Giving way to warmth and to light

In May, Don went to Ontario to see his brother who was ailing and I stayed at his condo. He lives on Jasper Avenue and 124th Street only a few blocks from where Aunt Betty had her restaurant where I worked at ages fourteen and fifteen. I've always been drawn to the river valley since that time and when I first saw Don's condo, I couldn't believe it. It's built on the river banks and his windows look at the river and valley. I am grateful to be able to spend time there and access my beloved trails so easily. On an early morning walk, words showed up with a very strong vibration and I knew even as I wrote them that this poem was going to be for me and Don.

KARMA

The music touches her soul deeply
As they step out onto the floor
It is here she feels their connection the strongest
And she could not ask for more
She knows that the depths of these feelings
He doesn't feel but still
There is an awareness deep within her
That with awakening he one day will
She understands that their meeting was a gift
And their destiny is to be as one
But there's fear hiding deep within
And it blocks all like clouds block the sun
She is no stranger to pain and to fear
Many times she's overcome them with love

She's always gone where she's been led
As she knows her directions come from above
She has always felt that inner light
And the visions have shown her the way
She knows and accepts that she is a messenger
But the fear sometimes wants her to stray
Away from her current commitments
Away from what she can see
That the pain will be beyond what she's felt
If he cannot get to where he must be
But deep inside she knows she won't leave
The love and the LIGHT will help her to stay
The future she knows will unfold as it will
It has always been this way
He is here to be her anchor
Her comfort and her guide
She can trust in him and somehow knows
That they will always walk side by side

This poem is very personal and at first I had no intention of sharing it. However once again I was guided to include it.

August 2012 found Don and I back in P.E.I. for his family reunion. I had the poem "Coming Home" put in the local newspaper in celebration of the family reunion but never told anyone including Don. He was surprised when people kept coming up to him and asking if his girlfriend was the poet who wrote the poem in the paper. He was happy that I had done this for the family and wanted me to read it to everyone after one of the get-togethers. The answer to that was a quick and simple, "NO WAY!" The end of 2012 found us once again planning a trip back to Puerto Vallarta, this time with an agenda for myself, to start the rough draft of the book.

2013

Woke up one morning early in January knowing that 2013 was going to be a year of challenges on many levels. I had feelings of an ending and of a beginning. I saw doors and windows closing to signify endings of many different contracts. Then I saw curtains blowing in an open window and a rainbow in the sky signifying new beginnings and spiritual growth.

I spent three weeks in Mexico in February and March working on the rough draft for the book every day. By the end of the third week, I had the rough draft done. It was an interesting process. I took three hours every morning and sat on a lounger until it became uncomfortable, then moved to a table and chair. The words flowed as soon as my pencil hit the paper. What was also interesting was the number of people stopping to ask what I was writing and how could I write without stopping to think. I had many interruptions; however, it resulted in some interesting conversations.

May found a good friend facing more struggles. It is hard to watch someone you care for trying to make sense out of what is happening in his or her life but none of us can walk the path for another. We are each unique in our humanness and the greatest gift we can give one another is love and respect for each other while we pursue our purpose. While on our journeys there are spiritual contracts that we enter into and most of us are unaware of these. They are contracts with certain people placed on our paths and they can be very short or a lifetime long. There is a saying, "We meet for a reason, a season, or a lifetime." These contracts can cover many different kinds of relationships. It could be a friendship, a partnership, a marriage, a teacher,a student, and so forth. What is important to understand and accept is that they all fulfill a purpose whether it be for a reason, season, or lifetime and once that purpose has been fulfilled, the contracts are finished.

Events come to be, unfold, and end on the spiritual plain far before they do on the earth plain. Long before we break out of a relationship, we know on a subliminal level that it is finished but it sometimes takes awhile for us to understand and accept the truth of it. It is important that we honor both ourselves and the others on our path and part of that honor is in letting go of a relationship or contract that has ended. Should we not be able to see this for ourselves or be able to make the break ourselves, the universe will do it for us and this is not the way we want anything to end since it is usually a very hard and hurtful lesson.

Relationships are joyful and important to our lives only when they enhance or shift our own inner wisdom. We need to trust, value, and respect one another when we enter into a relationship and it is critical to both parties that we do the same when we end a relationship. If we cannot understand and do this we will be limited in our spiritual growth.

Towards the end of May, a poem appeared one morning

as I was out walking. Once I read it, I knew it was meant for my close friend, Caroline. Caroline is Shari's sister and like Shari is beautiful inside and out. It hurts me when someone I'm close to is in pain since I can feel it as well but can't do the work they must do in order to be happy and free. When I had time I copied the poem onto a photo of her when she was smiling and happy and gave it to her when we met for a coffee. It is a poem filled with truth for all of us.

UNFOLDING

The Chapters of a person's life
Unfold as the decades do
The ninth year is a finishing time
And zero marks beginning anew
You cannot add more water
To a glass that overflows

To embrace the present you must finish the past
As that is how your future grows
The only thing that holds you back
From a future you are destined to explore
Are the untruths that keep you grounded in fear
And the damaging thoughts you cannot ignore
The doorway has been opening
And it is only you who can step thru
Embrace all that is within your grasp
The LIGHT and the Truth are within you

June saw my oldest grandson graduate and saw me wondering where the hell the years went and how could I possibly be as old as I was when inside I was still young! A couple of months before Kieran's graduation day I wondered if I could "order" a poem. Everyday I asked my angels and guides to send me a poem Nothing showed up so I finally gave up and decided I would have to write something myself. I did manage to write a poem but it was flat and had no emotion or connection to Kieran. So I decided I'd need to find a special card for him. A few nights before the big day I had dreams of Kieran from a baby to young adult and of all the times we spent together.

I got to hold him soon after his birth and all of the emotions I felt were there in the dream. Since he was the first grandchild we spent lots of time together. After I was on my own, we took several driving trips to Vancouver and had some wonderful times. The dream was a treasure chest of beautiful memories played out like a movie. The next morning as I was eating breakfast the words started to come and I started writing.

When I went back to read what I wrote I felt all of

the emotions from the dream washing over me like a huge wave. Of all the poems that have come to me, I felt this one the strongest because this was a part of my life. A part of me lived in Kieran and would continue to live within him long after I was gone.

I was unsure about putting this into the book but I realized that someday, some place a parent, grandparent or great-grandparent could read these words and feel what I felt and understand the words because they had also lived them. I understood that it wasn't only me this poem was gifted to, it was for anyone who was a parent, grandparent or great grandparent. As I have been writing this I have felt my mom and dad's presence with me. Beautiful, beautiful!! One thing this experience taught me was that there is no "poetry on demand channel."

YESTERDAY

Seems like only yesterday
I held you, all wrapped in blue
To me you were so small and special
That moment I've always held onto
Seems like only yesterday
I saw my mothers eyes; so proud
You were the first great grandchild

So happy, healthy and loud
Seems like only yesterday
I bounced you on my knee
I blinked my eyes and turned around
Already you were three
Seems like only yesterday
You were playing with stones and sticks
And before I'd gotten used to three
You were already six
Seems like only yesterday
We were on adventures you and me
The fun we had as we enjoyed our trips
Were great treasures then and will always be
Seems like only yesterday
I bounced you on my knee
Today you're a high school graduate
Now make your world what you want it to be

July I took my oldest granddaughter to Vancouver with
a stop in Kelowna on the way. We spent time with Shari
and Rhiannon was really impressed that we had been best
friends for over fifty years although "fifty" meant nothing to
her since she was only eleven. This was my opportunity to
make memories with her the same as I had done with Kieran.
Our visit with Shannon, Lesa, and Regan was filled with fun
and adventure and most importantly, memories!!! During
this time I found myself to be free from all commitments
both earthbound and spiritual, no visions and no poems,
just my family.

There are times when I sit quietly at home with just my
music in the background and think of my family, friends,
and the people who have been placed on my path both in

the past and present. A beautiful bouquet of flowers comes to my mind, all unique in their own beauty, strength, and purpose. I am filled with a deep sense of gratitude for what I had and now have in my life.

December was a month filled with visions and messages and a feeling of closure. I had a meeting with a well known psychic earlier in the year and she confirmed what I was feeling and "seeing." She explained that I had a thirteen year cycle coming to an end which certainly explained the kind of year I was having. Mid-December found me Christmas shopping at West Edmonton Mall with my friend Rennaye. We had gone early to try to avoid the crowds but it was still busy and we kept getting interrupted with my having to stop to write. Rennaye had the opportunity to see how these poems came to be.

When I finally got back to my office, I printed the poem on Word and sent her a copy. It was a very powerful poem for myself and when I asked Rennaye what it said to her, she told me that she saw me finishing whatever I was meant to do and a new purpose was unfolding.

JUST DANCE

Shall I dance in sunrise light
Or shall I dance in moon light bright
Will it be on a sandy beach
Or on a shady path just out of reach
Perhaps on a grassy dew kissed lawn
When birds are singing and welcoming dawn
Or it could be on a cobbled street
Where ancient stone and modern meet
It could be under a clear blue sky
Or there could be dark clouds floating by
I might be kissed by the hot sun
Or showered with rain as my day is done
I will dance with the trees that sway in time
To the breeze and the music in my mind
Where ever I find myself to be

I shall dance in celebration of being free
I will drink a toast to all I hold dear
And I shall dance to the music that only I hear

The freedom that the poem speaks of has nothing to do with being in a relationship and everything to do with being in the right relationship both with someone else and with yourself. It is about knowing who you are, being who you are, loving who you are, accepting others as they are, and having others accept you as you are. It is about not owing anyone anything and not expecting anything from anyone. It is about living in the now, letting go of the past, and not dwelling on the future. Most important, it is about celebration of unity with the Divine. On Dec twenty-sixth I set out on a long hike in the river valley since it was a beautiful warm, windless day. I stopped often to record the words of a poem and to just experience the sensations that were with me that day. Again, as in the start of the year, I was sensing doors and windows closing; sensing a weight lifting off my shoulders; and sensing a bright light around my body. At times I felt the *kundalini* energy again running from the base of my spine to my crown chakra which was vibrating like it never had done before. At one point, I had a very vivid vision of hands setting me gently on a dirt path. This was very powerful bringing tears and a few people stopped to see if I was okay. I finally got back to the condo and to a glass of wine that was waiting for me. I had a strong sense that this would be the last poem for awhile and was meant for all who would come to read it.

THE JOURNEY

Tis a magical journey that we take
From the womb unto the grave
We will be blessed by LIGHT and blessed by dark
Depending on the energies we gave
Calm seas do not a good sailor make
And this is true of life
We cannot reach the richest of rich
On a path not peppered with strife
Our lives are constantly changing
And often this is something we don't see
We hang onto beliefs and people and the past
When what we need to do is set them free
The darkness will always be followed by LIGHT
And we need to understand and fully accept
That darkness is our teacher and we can learn
The wisdom of knowing what to keep and what to reject
The biggest mistake that we'll make on this journey

From the womb unto the grave
Will not be what we choose to release
Or what we choose to save
The mistake will be how we made these choices
Often made in anger or in fear
And we unwisely choose with our heads
       and with our hearts
Instead of with Spirit whose purpose is clear
It is our Spirit that knows the truth of us
And it's from the wisdom of Spirit that we must
       learn to choose
For it's our minds and our emotions that deceive us
And in the end we lose
This also is a lesson we must learn
That there is nothing that does not teach
There is no wrong choice or wrong path
Just decisions putting purpose further from our reach
Tis a long journey from head and heart to soul
And this is one lesson we must learn and keep
That the knowledge we need to grow and evolve
Comes from a place within us deep

As I read the poem again I was struck by the power of it. It speaks of being blessed not only by the Light but also by the Darkness and further on it mentions that there is nothing that does not teach. It also speaks of the need to let go of people, beliefs, and the past which most of us have a hard time doing or we do it in anger or fear which hurts us even more. I had a strong feeling that this poem marked the end of the cycle which began when my mom died. 2014 would be a time for more "house cleaning" and the time to finish the book I had been working on for so long.

2014

By spring of 2014, I had a sense of being more grounded and at the same time, freer. The heaviness I felt for the past several years was lifting. The absence of one thing creates the presence of another; one finishes and one begins. The past thirteen years had been intense. I lost both mother and father and then husband and a thirty-four year marriage within a four year period.

I gained personal freedom and incredible spiritual growth which often left me overwhelmed and exhausted. I came to understand that the two biggest inhibitors to spiritual growth were fear and judgment, neither of these fall under the domain of the LIGHT. While we are entitled to our own opinions, we must be very careful that our thoughts, words and actions do not cross the line into judgment. For as long as I can remember I've had a reminder whenever I judged someone or something. "Judge not lest ye be judged," comes to me and I apologize to the universe and ask God for forgiveness. I have always assumed that this warning comes from the same place that my other messages do and am grateful and humbled.

During this thirteen year cycle I was even more aware of the miracles happening all around me and I know that the key to this world of miracles is belief. The more I work with the universe the more the universe works with me. There are many old sayings that support this truth. "What goes around comes around," and "you reap what you sow" are two of them and are full of truth.

When we see and are grateful for the miracles around us and already in our lives, we are blessed with more.. If we are constantly looking for more, we can't see what we already have and this is a huge problem in our culture. I don't believe in accidents or coincidence, I do believe in purpose. This brings to mind a quote from Einstein, "God does not play dice with the world." When we live with purpose we do not see "accidents" or "coincidence," we see miracles. The more we see and acknowledge the universe working with and for us, the more the miracles unfold and the closer we become to the source of all. There is no better place to be while we are here!!!

In February a good friend lost her father and when she called to tell me I was getting ready to take my grandkids home. As soon as I hung up the phone the poem, "A Girl's Best Friend" came to mind and I thought that I would give a copy of it to Halina. As I was driving my grandkids back to their mom's, I had words come to mind so I pulled over to write them down.

As soon as I finished writing, a melody came to mind and I found myself singing "A Girl's Best Friend" with the new words in the middle of the poem. I was really surprised at this as it never happened before and I was concerned I would forget the melody. When I finally got back home I rewrote "A Girl's Best Friend" to include the additional words and renamed it "Forever Near." It gave a whole new meaning to the poem and captured Halina's dad. I had met him and heard Halina speak of him many times. The new words reflected what I had known of him which was very touching. The melody came back to me and I found myself singing the poem which had now become a song. This and "Lynn's Song" are the only two poems that ever came with a melody.

FOREVER NEAR

You cannot see me
But I'm still here
While you are grieving
I'll stay very near
You can grieve for me
For a little while
Then let me go
Remember me with your smile

I'll be the robins song
I'll be the morning breeze
I'll be the flowers scent
From your apple trees
I'll be your gardens bloom
But I won't fade away
I'll be with you still
Forever and a day
I'll be with you
In the morning sun
And I'll be with you
When your day is done
Let me rest
With the flowers bright
I'll be with you still
With each new light

By summer's end my relationship with Don had come to
an end as well. We both knew that our purpose for meeting
was fulfilled and it was time to end the relationship but
never an easy thing to do. Fortunately he is a very old
soul and a wise man. We were able to end the relationship
without damaging the friendship that we both valued so
much. Friendships such as this are hard to come by and we
both know it and treat it with the respect it deserves.

By this time no more poems came to me and I began
to think they had come to an end. I continued to do some
"house cleaning" in my mind and spent as much time as
possible outside. I had images of empty rooms and doors
and windows opening which told me that a whole new
cycle was coming.

The visions continued and they were all of myself in an

ancient time and place. I also started having sensations in both my hands that were new to me and hard to interpret. The first was a pressure on both palms in the shape of circles. It wasn't painful but I definitely felt it. When I looked at my palms, they appeared normal although the circles felt hot. In my mind I saw circles connected into shapes that were unusual to me but seemed to have a lot of power. The circles continued for several months and when I asked Bill about them he had no answers for me.

In the fall the images changed from circles to triangles and in my mind I saw three sided triangles.. There was no pain but like the circles the image was hot. Along with the images of triangles in my mind came the words "power of three." I have no idea what this means and so far have not been guided to any answers but often three comes to my mind. The circles and triangles show up for a few days and then are gone for weeks, leaving me with questions and no answers. I trust that when the time is right I will find out their purpose

2014 is drawing to an end and no new poems have come to me, so I believe that now is the time to set them free. I have been told many times that they were not for me to keep; that I was simply the instrument to bring them to light. There are two purposes for this book; one has been to set the poems free, and I have fulfilled that purpose. The other is to share my experiences with others who are searching for purpose and who have possibly had similar experiences. Where I go from here, I don't know. I do know that wherever I go, I go with God. On December twenty-fourth my intention was to print this book and give it to Bill to proofread but I kept receiving the message, "not done yet" so I finally closed up my computer and decided to have a hot bath before going to my daughter, Tara's, for Christmas Eve. As I was laying in the tub, my palms began burning with the triangle sign and the words "power of three" ran over and over in my mind. All of a sudden the words "power of three" were replaced with one word "trinity" and then the words

"Father, Son, and Holy Spirit;"then the words, "God, Jesus, and Virgin Mary."

As soon as these words came to me so did the Light and a huge sense of freedom along with tears. I had intuitively looked at my watch when the words "God, Jesus and Virgin Mary" came to me and the time was 3:48. This seemed to be very important so when I got out of the tub and dried off, I got pen and paper and wrote December 24, 2014, 3:48 then in numerology style which is 2 24 2014 3 48. In numerology a series of numbers are always added together then reduced to one number. When I added the numbers together and reduced them to one number the number was three. I was stunned and felt like time stopped. Everything seemed to be in a cloud of absolute stillness, it was a very eerie, surreal feeling. I finally shook my head to wake up and then fetched my Sacred Numbers book to look up the number three. I read, "The ascended Master Jesus is near. He hears your prayers and is with you and is responding to them." I started to cry and then I felt hands on my shoulders, peace settle over me, and the word "Amen" came to me.

Our lives are important, we are important and we need to know that deep inside. Our life is God's gift to us; what we do with this life is our gift to God. We don't want to be an extra in the movie of our own lives. We don't all live our lives in the same way. Some of us come here to make a big impact; we are "bigger than life" and are noticed and impact the lives of many. Others of us do not want to be noticed. We are quiet people doing what we believe in and live our lives in a much simpler way.

There is no life more valuable than another since we are all here for the purpose of evolving. All life is precious to God and we all contribute in some way to the greater picture. It is not always the "larger than life" people who make the biggest contribution. It is the quiet, dedicated teacher who has that rare gift of truly connecting with the student that passes on the gift of learning and knowledge. They will be remembered by the students whose lives they altered and while they may not be noticed by the world, the difference they make in the world, through the student, is immeasurable.

Sometimes it is the most unexpected people who have the biggest impact on the lives of many. This brings to mind the book, Conversations With God which was written by a homeless man. We are all connected, all part of the whole, all important, all precious, and all God's masterpieces in the jig saw puzzle of life.

We humans are the sum of many parts. Some are easy to discern but others are not. The "others" are still very much a part of our total being; we have just hidden them in one of our many inner "rooms" until we have the capacity to deal with them. We become happier, healthier, and wiser when we can open these "rooms" and do some serious cleaning. If we can't find the strength and perseverance needed to clean these rooms, we'll not grow and evolve. We can do none of this if we're not even aware that such rooms exist.

Awakening is a slow process and takes much inner work to reach the capacity to begin to understand. Answers are to be found everywhere; the environment of our early years, our birth sign, our birth number, our Karmic ties and obligations. All contribute answers as to who we are. We may choose not to believe in any of this but that choice doesn't negate the Truth that lies within us all.

My life has been blessed with visions, messages, meetings, and the touch of the *Divine*. I have shared a few of them for the purpose of this book.

I have been advised by my messengers that all of the ascended Masters have been re-incarnated to this planet Earth to be with us at this time. The times in which we are now living have been spoken of in all of the Holy Books of every major religion on the planet. Not all technology has taken us towards the Light; but like all addictions it has taken us away from being in control of our own minds and from thinking for ourselves. It is imperative; in these times; that we align ourselves with the Light and it is imperative that WE, not our addictions, have control of our minds and we are thinking for ourselves.

CPSIA information can be obtained
at www.ICGtesting.com
Printed in the USA
LVOW04s0109030616

491026LV00015B/73/P